Play and Imagination
in Children with Autism

Play and Imagination
in Children with Autism

SECOND EDITION

PAMELA J. WOLFBERG

Teachers College
Columbia University
New York and London

Autism Asperger Publishing Company
www.asperger.net

Autism Asperger
Publishing Company
Overland Park, Kansas

Published simultaneously by Teachers College Press, 1234 Amsterdam Avenue, New York, NY 10027, Autism Asperger Publishing Company, 15490 Quivira Road, Overland Park, KS 66221.

Library of Congress Cataloging-in-Publication Data

Wolfberg, Pamela J.
  Play and imagination in children with autism / Pamela J. Wolfberg. — 2nd ed.
     p. cm.
  Includes bibliographical references and index.
  ISBN 978-0-8077-4941-8 (pbk : alk. paper) — ISBN 978-0-8077-4942-5 (cloth : alk. paper)
    1. Autistic children—Education—California—Longitudinal studies. 2. Autism in children—California—Longitudinal studies. 3. Play—California—Longitudinal studies. 4. Imagination in children—California—Longitudinal studies. 5. Skills in children—California—Longitudinal studies. I. Title.

  LC4718.5.C2W65 2009
  371.94—dc22

                        2008051220

ISBN: 978-0-8077-4941-8 (paper)
ISBN: 978-0-8077-4942-5 (cloth)

Printed on acid-free paper
Manufactured in the United States of America

16   15   14   13   12   11   10   09   8   7   6   5   4   3   2   1

To "Teresa," "Freddy," and "Jared,"
whose passage to children's play culture
is revealed within these pages

and

to my mother, who inspired
my life's work with her passion for art
and enriching the lives of children in need

Contents

Preface

I WAS DELIGHTED when I received an invitation to write a revised second edition of *Play and Imagination in Children with Autism*. Admittedly, I had not read my book since it was published nearly a decade ago. When I did so, I was astounded to discover that while a great deal has changed in the field of autism, most of the ideas I originally proposed have continued to guide my research and practice to date. At first, I felt conflicted with this realization; it was not clear to me whether I should rejoice or shrink away in despair for not having had any major epiphanies in all this time. Upon further reflection, I felt encouraged, recognizing that the evolution of my life's *play-work* is rooted in a basic perspective that is sufficiently well grounded.

The major aims of this book remain virtually the same as those of the original—to advance what we know and can do to address the complex issues that children on the autism spectrum encounter in social and imaginary play. Most of what I amended speaks to the significant new developments that have transpired in the field of autism. I have scoured the literature for the most recent and relevant information on theory, research, and practice, including that which is reflected in the Integrated Play Groups (IPG) model. Readers will note that while I have added many new references (some of which have replaced older ones) I have also retained many of the "classic" references, which have withstood the test of time.

This book remains the cornerstone on which continued efforts to develop inclusive peer play programs for children with autism have been built. Shortly after the publication of the original work, the Autism Institute on Peer Relations and Play was founded to advance research, training, and practice in this area. The IPG model has since flourished, through the collective efforts of many remarkable professionals, family members, and the children themselves. Now widely considered an empirically supported intervention, the IPG model has been adopted by numerous schools and organizations at the local, national, and international level. Further, its original principles and practices have led to the development of new approaches that address a wide range of ages and abilities, while incorporating such innovations as sensory integration, art, drama, film, and other special interests defined by the players. While training seminars and curriculum materials are also available, this book is recommended as the first of required readings for anyone who is serious about learning how to apply the practices of the IPG model.

This book is directed to those with an interest in children on the autism spectrum, most notably in the areas of play and imagination, peer relations, and childhood culture. It may be especially relevant to educators, therapists, researchers, and family members, as well as adults who identify themselves as being on the autism spectrum.

Notable additions have been made throughout the first six chapters. Chapter 1 provides an introduction that highlights the evolution of the IPG model and research to date, while the major areas to be explored are framed in subsequent chapters. In Part I a variety of theoretical and practical viewpoints are discussed. Chapter 2 examines the nature of autism from past to present with major updates on incidence, diagnosis, and characteristics. Chapter 3 offers various historical and theoretical perspectives on the nature of play. Chapter 4 compares and contrasts play's natural course in typical development with play variations in children with autism. Chapter 5 bridges the gap between theory and practice, with a current review of play interventions and description of the IPG model.

Part II presents the ethnographic case portraits of Teresa, Freddy, and Jared, who faced significant challenges entering into the "play culture" of their peers. Chapters 6 through 11 represent different periods in Teresa, Freddy, and Jared's development, with particular attention given to the time they participated in Integrated Play Groups. Within these chapters I describe each child's social relations with peers, transformations in play, and transformations in words and pictures. Weaving together rich description, dialogue, and examples of writing and drawing, I strive to bring the children's stories to life.

In the final chapter I attempt to bring focus to the major questions explored, proposing possible explanations for Teresa, Freddy, and Jared's patterns of social and symbolic growth. The implications of what I discovered are discussed in terms of contemporary theories of autism and new and future directions in research and practice.

Acknowledgments

I WISH TO THANK the many people who made this book possible. I am deeply indebted to the children portrayed in these pages, for allowing me to enter their play worlds and bring their stories to life. My heartfelt thanks also go to their families and schools, whose understanding and generosity were instrumental to this work.

I am especially grateful to Adriana Schuler and James Stone for their patience, encouragement, and thoughtful commentary; Rebecca Berry, Kristen Bottema, Joseph Campione, Mila DeWitt, Glenda Fuge, Jean Gonsier-Gerdin, Susan Janko, Heather McCracken, Lorraine McCune, David Neufeld, Kathryn Orfirer, Charles Peck, Suzanne Pemberton, and Tara Tuchel for helpful comments that challenged and shaped my past and present thinking; and Cerrissa MacNichols, Emily Burnell Petrou, Jane Schisgal, and Craig Zercher for their assistance while conducting research.

I wish to express my appreciation to the Glenna B. Collins Scholarship Foundation of the Autism Society of America and the Sandra L. Bailey Memorial Fund of the Illinois Autism Society for their generous contributions.

I also wish to thank Brian Ellerbeck, Karl Nyberg, Susannah Driver, and Lyn Grossman at Teachers College Press for thoughtful reading of the manuscript, sensitive and careful editing, and seeing this work through to completion.

My deepest gratitude goes to Therese O'Connor, whose beautiful spirit and passion lives on in guiding my life's play-work.

Finally, I am eternally grateful to Axel and Luna for their unwavering support, friendship, and love throughout this venture.

CHAPTER 1

Overview

We were taught to say that play is the work of children. But, watching and listening to them, I saw that play was nothing less than Truth and Life.
—Vivian Paley, *The Boy Who Would Be a Helicopter: The Uses of Storytelling in the Classroom*

THIS BOOK EXPLORES the social and imaginary lives of three extraordinary children, whom I call Teresa, Freddy, and Jared.* I initially came to know these children as students in my special education class in an urban elementary school in northern California. They had been diagnosed with an autism spectrum disorder, a perplexing condition that affects development in a number of distinct ways. Ten years had passed since the enactment of the Education for All Handicapped Children Act of 1975 (reauthorized as the Individuals with Disabilities Education Act [IDEA] in 1997/2004), which established the right of children with disabilities to be educated alongside typically developing peers within the least restrictive environment. Once destined for the locked wards of state institutions, Teresa, Freddy, and Jared represented a new generation of children with autism to be educated in the public schools.

Although I had previously worked with atypical populations, this was my first experience as a teacher of children with autism. Admittedly, I was somewhat naive in my understanding of the condition and effective instructional practices that were known at the time. My image of the child with autism was simplistic at best—detached, isolated, in a world apart, preoccupied with unusual interests, and sometimes possessed of remarkable talents. I also had a vague notion that autism was somehow linked to a dysfunction in the brain and that the once-popular "blame the mother"

---

*All names of people, schools, and locations have been changed to protect the privacy of those involved.

theories had become passé. Still, it wasn't clear to me what impact these notions had on the education and treatment of children with autism. To my knowledge, practitioners greatly varied in orientation, drawing on behavioral, developmental, or psychotherapeutic techniques.

I knew that I had much to learn if I was to become an effective special educator with this unique population of children. To prepare myself, I enrolled in the master's program at San Francisco State University, where I was fortunate to study under Professor Adriana Schuler, a well-known expert in the area of communication and autism. She was a gold mine of current information on autism, digging ever deeper into theoretical and practical issues.

Over time I was able to absorb and integrate this new knowledge with my past experience with children. I had previously encountered children from all walks of life while working in a variety of educational programs and traveling around the world. As a special educator, I primarily worked with children labeled "severely emotionally disturbed" (some of whom I later discovered were misdiagnosed and actually were on the autism spectrum) in residential and day treatment facilities. An extension of this work included training as a play therapist under the direction of an expert clinician. While traveling, I had the good fortune to work and live among typically developing children from many different countries. I was an "ethnographer" in the making as I closely observed and documented children's everyday life and patterns of sociocultural activity. These diverse experiences ultimately shaped the direction of my research and practice with children on the autism spectrum, which now has become a lifelong passion.

PROBLEMS CHILDREN WITH AUTISM EXPERIENCE IN PLAY

I grew to appreciate the complex nature of autism while working with Teresa, Freddy, and Jared. Autism is characterized by qualitative impairments in reciprocal social interaction, communication, and imagination and by the presence of restricted, repetitive, and stereotyped patterns of behavior, interest, and activities (American Psychiatric Association, 2000). Paucity of spontaneous play is a distinct characteristic of autism, one not easily disentangled from cognitive, social, and affective aspects of the disorder.

I was especially concerned with how seriously impoverished Teresa, Freddy, and Jared were in their play and how isolated they were from their peer culture. They encountered significant problems in pretending and in coordinating social activity with peers. This was consistent with a growing collection of research on play and social development in children with autism.

Research shows that children with autism have specific impairments in spontaneous symbolic play that may extend to functional play (for reviews, see Baron-Cohen, 1987; Harris, 1993; Jarrold, 2003; Jarrold, Boucher, & Smith, 1993; Libby, Powell, Messer, & Jordan, 1998; Williams, Reddy, & Costall, 2001). Children with autism gravitate to repetitive play activity, ranging from manipulating objects and enacting elaborate routines to pursuing obsessive and narrowly focused interests. Without specific guidance, they are less likely to play with objects in a functional manner. Moreover, they rarely produce pretend play by transforming objects; activating dolls as agents; or inventing imaginary objects, roles, and events. Qualities of diversity, flexibility, and creativity are visibly absent in play activity.

Similarly, children with autism lack a predisposition to spontaneously play with peers (Carter, Davis, Klin, & Volkmar, 2005; Dissanayake, Sigman, & Kasari, 1996; Howlin, 1986; Jordan, 2003; Lord, 1984; Sigman & Ruskin, 1999). In free-play situations, they typically avoid peers or resist social overtures, passively enter play with little or no self-initiation, or approach peers in an obscure and one-sided fashion (Wing & Gould, 1979). Overall, children with autism direct fewer initiations to peers in unstructured settings. When they do approach peers, they seldom convey and interpret social communicative signals in ways that normally facilitate successful play entry and coordination of actions. The task of coordinating play with peers in a social pretend framework is particularly complex, since children with autism do not spontaneously comprehend and produce imaginative play.

PLAY'S PURPOSE AND PLACE IN CHILDHOOD

My concern for Teresa, Freddy, and Jared deepened as I contemplated the role of play in childhood culture and development. I recalled my observations of children playing while traveling. I was struck by the consistency with which children of diverse ages and abilities from around the globe constructed unique play worlds separate from adults and by how each play world reflected the tools, activities, and themes of their society and culture. I also recalled my experiences as a play therapist with a little girl who had severe emotional problems. In my presence, she constructed a make-believe world in which she played out her personal struggles with dolls and puppets as her confidants. This made me wonder about play's universal purpose and place in the life of children as well as its conspicuous absence in children with autism.

While history has shown that perceptions of play's purpose and place in childhood are forever shifting with the Zeitgeist, there is abundant literature documenting play's significance for children's learning, development, and sociocultural participation (Elkind, 2007; Fromberg & Bergen, 2006; Isenberg & Quisenberry, 2002; Singer, Golinkoff, & Hirsh-Pasek, 2006; Wolfberg, 2005). Specifically, research links play (with both objects and people) to advances in cognitive, social, communicative, linguistic, and emotional development. Exploratory play is associated with a child's growing understanding of the functions and meanings of objects. Symbolic play, involving transformations of objects, contributes to the development of logic, memory, and abstract thinking (Piaget, 1962; Vygotsky, 1966, 1978). Social play fulfills a number of interrelated social cognitive functions that are necessary for developing social competence and forming mutual friendships (Rubin & Thompson, 2003).

Social pretend play is an especially important vehicle for socialization and the appropriation of social and cultural knowledge (Bretherton, 1984; Bruner, 1990; Vygotsky, 1966, 1978). Within a social pretend framework, children imitate, observe, and integrate progressively complex actions and roles to achieve interpersonal coordination in play. While collaborating on play scripts, they mutually explore social roles and issues of intimacy, trust, negotiation, and compromise (Dunn, 2004; Howes, Unger, & Matheson, 1992; Rubin & Thompson, 2003). Children also master communication in social pretend play by constructing a shared understanding of literal and nonliteral meaning (Bretherton, 1984; Garvey, 1977). This underlies the child's growing awareness and appreciation of the perspectives of others, and the adoption of a metarepresentational mode, capacities seen as critical for socialized thought (Boucher & Wolfberg, 2003).

Considering play's pivotal role in the process of socialization and the attainment of social and symbolic understanding, I wondered whether problems in play might be at the core of the autistic condition and experience. In other words, the lack of spontaneous social reciprocity and symbolic representation in play may be viewed not only as signs or symptoms of autism, but also as obstacles to developing and participating in play. As will be discussed in subsequent chapters, the social, communication, and imaginative features that define autism are now being viewed through a number of theoretical lenses that may offer insight into both the causes and consequences of impaired play.

CAPACITIES FOR SYMBOLIC AND SOCIAL PLAY

Unraveling the myriad problems children with autism experience in play continues to be one of the most significant challenges facing theorists, practitioners, and family members. A critical question posed in my earlier work is whether children with autism have capacities for symbolic and social play that they do not spontaneously exhibit in free-play conditions. Conclusions may be drawn from a seminal body of research.

Initial experimental and observational studies demonstrated noteworthy outcomes for children with autism when supported in play with adults and peers in structured settings. With respect to symbolic play, early studies have shown that children with autism are capable of comprehending and producing more sophisticated forms of play (functional, symbolic, or both) and diverse play when elicited by an adult (Boucher & Lewis, 1990; Charman & Baron-Cohen, 1997; Jarrold et al., 1996; Lewis & Boucher, 1988; Mundy, Sigman, Ungerer, & Sherman, 1986; Riguet, Taylor, Benaroya, & Klein, 1981; Sigman & Ungerer, 1984). Similar findings have been reported in elicited conditions with both adults and typical peers present in inclusive play settings (Lord, 1984; McHale, 1983; Wolfberg & Schuler, 1993). Some studies have shown that children with autism, relative to developmentally matched peers, produce less diverse functional play, fewer symbolic acts, and fewer doll-directed acts (Mundy et al., 1986; Riguet et al., 1981; Sigman & Ungerer, 1984). However, others have reported no detectable differences, suggesting that children with autism are capable of producing "genuine" pretend play with minimal prompting and props (Boucher & Lewis, 1990; Charman & Baron-Cohen, 1997; Jarrold, Boucher, & Smith, 1996; Lewis & Boucher, 1988).

With respect to social play, preliminary studies mainly derive from early peer intervention research. A number of studies documented increases in rates of social initiations and responses using highly directed adult prompting procedures in peer play settings (Haring & Lovinger, 1989; Odom & Strain, 1986; Ragland, Kerr, & Strain, 1978; Strain, 1984; Strain, Kerr, & Ragland, 1979). Other investigations that elicited play with less intrusive procedures yielded improvements in the frequency, duration, and quality of social play (Casner & Marks, 1984; Lord, 1984; Lord & Hopkins, 1986; McHale, 1983; Wolfberg & Schuler, 1993).

The general conclusion drawn from these original studies is that with social support, children with autism have the potential to show greater competence (quantitatively and qualitatively) in both representational and social forms of play. This formative body of research paved the way for new and innovative approaches to studying and supporting children with autism in play.

CREATING THE INTEGRATED PLAY GROUPS MODEL

Since play is critical to a child's growing capacity to understand and relate to the social world, and ultimately to participate in the culture of play with peers, providing opportunities for children with autism to become competent in play is of prime importance. The challenge before me was to fashion a program that would enhance Teresa, Freddy, and Jared's social and symbolic play capabilities while fostering their full participation in normalized peer cultural activities. It seemed reasonable that such a program would need to occur in a socially integrated setting and correspond to natural play contexts.

In my early review of the intervention literature, I discovered that play (particularly with peers) had a relatively small role in the education and treatment of children with autism. The fact that play is notoriously difficult to operationally define and measure may partially explain its limited application. While many social skills programs at the time recognized play as a meaningful context for instruction, few deliberately targeted play as an area of competence. The few interventions that did attempt to teach play greatly varied in method and orientation. While some interventions seemed quite effective in promoting certain aspects of play and social behavior, I found none to be comprehensive. Most appeared to operate without a coherent conceptual framework of how play naturally occurs and influences symbolic and social development in children with autism. These included highly structured interventions focusing on the acquisition of discrete skills through adult-directed versus child-centered activity, as well as those that are loosely structured based on the assumption that play is what children do when left to their own devices. Without a clear understanding and appreciation of the obstacles children with autism encounter in play, such interventions are not likely to tap into their full potential for play.

To sufficiently address the play needs of children with autism, I initiated what has come to be known as the Integrated Play Groups (IPG) model (for overviews, see Schuler & Wolfberg, 2000; Wolfberg, 1995a, 1995b, 2004; Wolfberg & Schuler, 1999, 2006). The conceptual design for the IPG model originally drew on my personal experience and growing knowledge of theory and empirically based practice. An initial motivation came from working in an environment where social integration or inclusion was an integral part of the school culture resulting from the efforts of an extremely talented group of teachers, therapists, and parents. In some respects, disability was seen as one dimension of the diversity that existed among children in this school. This inspired me to build a program that would bring together children with differing abilities, cultural identities, and social backgrounds for the purpose of play.

The writings of Russian psychologist Lev Vygotsky (1966, 1978) proved to be a major source of inspiration for developing the IPG model. Vygotsky regarded play as instrumental in a child's growing capacity for symbolic representation and social understanding. Vygotskian theory emphasizes social factors as mediating learning and development. Accordingly, developmental changes indicative of a child's cognitive capacity manifest first in the context of social interaction with adults and more capable peers, and later in independent activity. More experienced partners further maximize the child's potential by systematically adjusting their assistance to match or slightly exceed the level at which novices are able to independently perform.

The IPG model attempts to apply Vygotskian theory by focusing on "guided participation" in play, a concept described by Barbara Rogoff (1990) as the process through which children develop while actively participating in culturally valued activity with the guidance, support, and challenge of companions who vary in skill and status.

Integrated Play Groups specifically aim to support children with autism (novice players) in natural play experiences with more capable peer play partners (expert players). These children participate in small groups organized around play activities and themes that encourage social interaction, communication, and imagination (for example, construction, pretend, art, music, movement, interactive games). An adult (play guide) facilitates spontaneous, mutually enjoyed, and reciprocal play among children while expanding on each child's social and symbolic play repertoire. A further intent is for the children to come to mediate play activities with minimal or no adult guidance. Embedded in this model are methods for observing, interpreting, and building on children's play interests and social communicative abilities and for designing environments conducive to social and imaginative play.

RESEARCH ON INTEGRATED PLAY GROUPS

From age 9 to 11 years, Teresa, Freddy, and Jared participated in the pilot Integrated Play Groups (IPG) program under my guidance. I received a small grant from a community educational foundation with which to purchase play materials and conduct a study. For this study, I collected extensive videotape footage documenting Teresa, Freddy, and Jared's early experiences in their respective play groups and related social activity. In a relatively short period of time, they each had progressed in their play with typically developing peers. This later became the subject of a video documentary I produced for my master's field study (Wolfberg, 1988).

My interest in Teresa, Freddy, and Jared's development extended beyond that of the IPG context. For each child, I put together a portfolio with various written documents and personal artifacts providing further evidence of their social and symbolic growth. Over time, I noted some rather remarkable transformations in their social relations with peers and symbolic representation in play, spoken language, writing, and drawing. Yet I had only begun to gather pieces of a mosaic that, once assembled, would tell the stories of these amazing children. Little did I know that I would have that opportunity as a qualitative researcher in the years to follow.

After Teresa, Freddy, and Jared graduated from elementary school, I entered into the joint doctoral program in special education at the University of California, Berkeley, with San Francisco State University. At the same time, Adriana Schuler and I codirected a research and demonstration project to further develop and refine the IPG model (Wolfberg & Schuler, 1992). We collaborated with a number of families and schools in the local community to set up Integrated Play Groups and field test the intervention model.

Building on these early efforts, a growing body of research focused on the IPG model has emerged over the years (Gonsier-Gerdin, 1992; Lantz, Nelson, & Loftin, 2004; Mikaelan, 2003; O'Connor, 1999; Richard & Goupil, 2005; Wolfberg, 1994; Wolfberg & Schuler, 1992, 1993; Yang, Wolfberg, Wu, & Hwu, 2003; Zercher, Hunt, Schuler, & Webster, 2001). This includes a series of exploratory and experimental studies conducted not only by our research team, but also by others who sought to replicate our work.

To date, the majority of studies have focused on the efficacy of the IPG model and its impact on the social and symbolic play dimensions of children with autism. Overall, studies have included children representing diverse ages (3 to 11 years) and abilities on the autism spectrum who participated in IPGs in school, home, and community settings in North America and Asia. Most of these studies also included social validation measures to assess parent perceptions of the impact of the intervention on their children with autism.

The accumulated findings suggest that as a whole the IPG model has been effective, yielding generalized and socially valued gains. With adult guidance and peer mediation, the children with autism showed higher levels of social and symbolic dimensions of play than exhibited prior to the implementation of the intervention. Specifically, decreases in isolate and stereotypic play were noted along with collateral gains in increasingly socially coordinated play (parallel, common focus, common goal) and representational play (functional and symbolic-pretend). Improvements in language were also documented in a few cases. Importantly, the research evidence also shows that the acquired skills were maintained when adult support was withdrawn. Further, observational and social validation data suggest that the acquired skills generalized beyond the specific play group to other peers and siblings, settings (school, home, community), and social activity contexts.

The attitudes, perceptions, and experiences of the expert players have also been explored (Gonsier-Gerdin, 1992; Wolfberg, 1994; Yang et al., 2003). On the basis of observations and interviews with the play guides and peers, it was reported that the peers developed greater sensitivity, tolerance, and acceptance of the novice players' individual differences. In addition, they articulated a sense of responsibility as well as an understanding of how to include the less skilled players by adapting to their different interests and styles of communication. They further reported having fun and developing mutual friendships with novice players that extended beyond the play group setting to after-school activities in the home and community.

While the IPG model has steadily gained recognition as an empirically supported intervention (Banks et al., 2005; DiSalvo & Oswald, 2002; Iovannone, Dunlop, Huber, & Kincaid, 2003), we acknowledge the need for ongoing research to address questions that as yet remain unanswered. In particular, the collected studies reported here are limited both in sample size and methodologies. One issue is that the population with autism is highly diverse, making it difficult to find a large number of participants who can be matched in comparable ways (National Research Council, 2001). Another issue is that the methodologies employed thus far do not provide direct evidence of the kinds of causal links afforded by traditional empirical studies involving controlled large-group experimental treatment designs. To that end, we are embarking on new long-term research that pairs two large-group studies that employ a randomized controlled design to examine the children with autism and qualitative inquiry to explore potential influences on the typical peers participating in IPGs (Wolfberg, Turiel, & DeWitt, in preparation). The strength of combining complementary methods opens up new research questions and avenues for study.

ETHNOGRAPHIC CASE PORTRAITS

Coming full circle, it was our pilot research that inspired me to look back at the experiences of Teresa, Freddy, and Jared for my doctoral dissertation. I had many questions and tentative hypotheses regarding the feasibility of enhancing play in children with autism, the qualitative processes underlying emerging capacities for reciprocal social relations and symbolic representation in play and related activity (spoken language, writing, and drawing), and the systems of social support that mediate social and symbolic growth.

This book derives from my doctoral dissertation, which explores how social relations and imagination naturally unfold in children with autism who are given support to play with peers (Wolfberg, 1994). I pursued a longitudinal study that followed the course of Teresa, Freddy, and Jared's development (from age 5 to 16 years), concentrating on the period during which they participated in IPGs (from age 9 to 11 years). I adopted an ethnographic case study approach, a form of qualitative inquiry grounded in the tradition of anthropology (Patton, 2002).

The decision to pursue ethnography derived from both theoretical and pragmatic considerations. Ethnography offered the best plan for exploring questions pertaining to the interactive processes of social and symbolic development based on the life experiences of a select and rare group of children. Focusing on the process of change rather than outcomes, sociocultural contexts rather than specific variables, and discovery rather than verification, this form of qualitative inquiry has intrinsic value for scientific research. A popular quote attributed to Einstein seems fitting to include here: "Not everything that can be counted counts, and not everything that counts can be counted."

Several features characterize the ethnographic case study approach adopted. A basic assumption is that meaning and process are embedded within culture and are essential to understanding human behavior. As participant-observer, the ethnographer is the key instrument for collecting, interpreting, and assembling a coherent understanding of the "data" gathered from multiple sources in the field. Inductive analysis steers the path of inquiry for the purpose of discovering relationships, generating hypotheses, and developing theory grounded in the data (Glaser & Strauss, 1967). "Thick and rich" description and visual accounts serve to illustrate emergent themes, hypotheses, and theory. Finally, applying "sophisticated rigor" through detailed description and triangulation offers quality assurance in the verification and application of methods (Denzin, 1978).

As an ethnographer, I participated in the community, school, classroom, and play cultures of which Teresa, Freddy, and Jared were a part. The challenge was to put myself inside the children's skin and view the world from their unique perspectives—as the Navajos put it, "To know me is to walk in my moccasins" (Stone & Gonsier-Gerdin, 1995).

The "data" I gathered consisted of videotapes, field notes, written documents, interviews, and personal artifacts (such as drawings, paintings, writing samples, letters, and photographs) drawn from each child's portfolio as well as additional sources. Through an inductive process, I analyzed this intricate network of information ultimately generating case portraits of Teresa, Freddy, and Jared's experiences.

In the remaining chapters I explore a series of questions that guided my thinking throughout this investigation. A first set of questions deals with the feasibility of establishing play in children with autism. Is there evidence to suggest the emergence of imaginative as well as socially coordinated play with peers? If so, what are the qualitative characteristics of these social and symbolic behavior changes, and how do they relate to each other in terms of timing and order of appearance? For instance, do social gains precede, parallel, or follow gains in functional or symbolic play? Are changes evident across domains indicative of symbolic growth (for example, spoken language, writing, and drawing)?

A related set of questions deals with the type of support, guidance, or instruction needed to bring about gains in play behavior. For instance, what is the adult's role in supporting social and symbolic growth? What is it that peers do to make them effective play partners? What types of social relationships evolve from peer play experiences? What is the group's experience in fostering inclusion and social cohesion?

SUMMARY

This introductory chapter highlights the evolution of the IPG model and research to date, while framing the major areas to be explored in subsequent chapters. Play's purpose and place in childhood is considered from both developmental and sociocultural viewpoints. Since impaired play is a core characteristic of the condition, this has profound implications for children with autism. There is evidence to suggest that children with autism may benefit from support to develop symbolic and social play. The IPG model was created to help address this area of need. To date, there is promising research on IPG, which has evolved to keep pace with rapid changes in the field. The ethnographic case portraits of Teresa, Freddy, and Jared are seminal to this body of work. In the following chapter, we examine the nature of autism to provide a context for understanding the experiences of these children.

P A R T I

Perspectives on Autism and Play

CHAPTER 2

The Nature of Autism

Maria, a 10-year-old girl with autism who had formerly participated in Integrated Play Groups, telephoned me after moving away with her family. Now that she was in a new environment, I wondered whether or not she still had the opportunity to play with other children. She informed me that she and her younger sister played together with dolls. Curious about the nature of this play, I asked her if she and her sister pretended with the dolls. Maria was quick to respond, "Oh yes, I pretend." But when I questioned her as to what she liked to pretend, Maria replied, "I don't know what pretend is, but I like to do it."

MARIA'S ENDEARING NAÏVETÉ personifies the unique and puzzling qualities associated with autism. While not every child with autism is as capable as Maria, she may well represent the voice of many. She expresses a genuine desire to be with, be like, and be accepted by her peers but has yet to fully comprehend the elusive world of their play culture. What is it that sets children with autism apart from the play of their peers? What can we do to bring them closer to these experiences? To explore these issues we must first consider the perspective of persons on the autism spectrum by examining the nature of this unique condition.

PIONEERS IN THE DISCOVERY OF AUTISM

More than a half century ago, Leo Kanner (1943) in Baltimore and Hans Asperger (1944) in Vienna independently, and unaware of each other, published remarkably similar accounts of two separate groups of children who had a number of unusual features in common. They each presented detailed case descriptions and generated hypotheses about the nature of this disorder. Both Kanner and Asperger speculated that in each of these cases, the appearance of characteristic problems originated in a basic disturbance present at birth. They noted an inability to form normal affective relationships as the most outstanding feature.

Both Kanner and Asperger even chose the term *autistic* to characterize the disorder, a label first introduced by the well-known psychiatrist Eugen Bleuler in 1911 to refer to a fundamental disturbance in schizophrenia (Frith, 2003). The terms *autistic* and *autism* derive from the Greek word *autos*, meaning "self." In reference to schizophrenia, Bleuler originally used the term *autistic* to describe a progressive withdrawal and loss of contact with the social world that was not present at birth. Stemming from this early usage, confusion over the terms *autism* and *schizophrenia* continued to be a problem. Today, *autism spectrum disorders* refers to a class of conditions that encompass both Kanner's and Asperger's discoveries.

Asperger's original article, published in German during World War II, remained largely unknown until it was translated into English by Uta Frith in 1992. Consequently, Kanner's seminal paper, "Autistic Disturbances of Affective Contact," published in *The Nervous Child*, became the most widely quoted in the literature. Asperger offered a wider definition of autism than did Kanner, including cases that ranged from severe impairment to near normal ability. *Asperger syndrome* presently refers to a subgroup within the autism spectrum presenting near-normal linguistic ability and intelligence. *Kanner's syndrome*, also known as *classic autism*, refers to a constellation of classic features based on Kanner's original observations of 11 children. These children all shared the following traits: preference for aloneness, obsessive insistence on sameness, liking of elaborate routines, and islets of ability.

Kanner considered "autistic aloneness" and "an obsessive insistence on sameness" to be defining features of the disorder. Influenced by the psychoanalytic perspective, which dominated the field at the time, he believed these to be deeply rooted psychological problems that could only be inferred from specific behaviors. He noted in all his cases that the children consistently ignored or shut out anything from the outside world. Most striking was their absence of two-way interactions with adults and peers. They had particular problems relating to peers and participating directly in their play activities. In contrast, these children seemed to relate well to physical objects and showed an interest in playing alone with them. Many of the children were drawn to books and acquired the skill to read; however, they had difficulty relating to characters and understanding the concept of story.

Kanner speculated that autistic children's behavior was governed not only by a desire for aloneness but also by an "anxiously obsessive" need to maintain sameness. They showed great distress when confronted with anything broken or incomplete. They insisted that actions and routines be carried out in a precise manner. This dread of incompleteness and change corresponded to repetitive language and action, resulting in a limited repertoire of spontaneous activity. Verbal utterances and patterns of activity were characteristically inflexible and unimaginative. These manifested in different ways, including making redundant stereotyped movements and vocalizations, carrying out elaborate routines, and pursuing obscure and narrowly focused interests.

In the years that followed Kanner's (1943) pioneering research, the study of autism diverged from his main conclusion that

> these children have come into the world with innate inability to form the usual biologically provided affective contact with people, just as other children come into the world with innate physical or intellectual handicaps. (p. 250)

In his final discussion, Kanner raised questions regarding the parents' possible influence on the psychological development of children with autism. He noted that the children he observed came from highly intelligent families, and he considered few of the fathers and mothers to be "warm-hearted." While he did not draw any specific conclusions, these allegations left an indelible impression on the theory and research that followed for at least 2 decades.

PSYCHOGENIC VERSUS BIOGENIC THEORIES

In the 1950s and 1960s, psychogenic theories came to the fore with the notion that overly intellectual and emotionally detached "refrigerator mothers" were to blame for driving their infants to withdraw into an autistic state (Bettelheim, 1967). This corresponded to the popularization of psychoanalytic approaches in the treatment of childhood psychiatric disorders. Symptomatic behaviors were thus interpreted as the child's logical and perhaps willful defense in coping with the ultimate rejection—an uncaring mother. The myth of the refrigerator mother clearly darkened the lives of many families, particularly mothers, with unfounded guilt.

Bernard Rimland (1964) played a significant role in confronting this blame-the-mother myth by postulating the organic nature of autism. Although traces of psychodynamic influences can still be found in the literature, most agree that the predilection to autism is biological.

Autism spectrum disorders is now considered a neurological condition that is influenced by both genetic variation and developmental factors (Sigman, Spence, & Wang, 2006). While there is no known single cause, research is focusing on potential links between genetics, heredity, and medical issues (Filipek, 2005; Minshew & Williams, 2008; Rutter, 2005). Studies show abnormalities in the structure and function of the brain that may be attributed to factors such as viral infections, birth complications, metabolic anomalies, environmental toxins, and genetic conditions. The evidence suggests that children are born with or predisposed to developing autism, but there are no definitive triggers. While autism is 2 to 4 times more prevalent in boys than in girls, it knows no other boundaries. Autism can affect any child and any family regardless of racial, ethnic, social, economic, educational, or cultural background.

INCIDENCE AND DIAGNOSIS

When I wrote the first edition of this book a decade ago, I could not have predicted the unprecedented increase in the number of children identified with autism. Throughout the world, autism has been on the rise and is continuing to grow at a rate reaching near-epidemic proportions. Ten years ago, 1 in 10,000 children was diagnosed with autism, while today estimates are as high as 1 in 150 (Centers for Disease Control, 2008). Based on these statistics, there are estimates of more than half a million cases in the United States. Since there are many people living with autism who do not have a formal diagnosis, it is likely that this number is actually much higher. While there appear to be multiple reasons why autism numbers are climbing (among them hereditary patterns, environmental factors), refined practices in detection, identification, and diagnosis contribute in large part (Fombonne, 2005).

Following their groundbreaking Camberwell study, Lorna Wing and Judith Gould (1979) introduced the "Triad of Impairments" (qualitative impairments in reciprocal social interaction, communication, and imagination), which has endured as key to an autism diagnosis. Two similar systems for diagnosing autism spectrum disorders are the *International Classification of Diseases* (ICD-10), prepared by the World Health Organization (1992), and the *Diagnostic and Statistical Manual of Mental Disorders* (DSM-IV-TR), issued by the American Psychiatric Association (1994, revised 2000). While both systems generally agree on the essential criteria for classification, they differ in their use of some terminology.

The DSM-IV-TR system classifies several subtypes of autism spectrum disorders within the category of pervasive developmental disorders (PDD).

These include autistic disorder, Rett's disorder, childhood disintegrative disorder, Asperger's disorder, and pervasive developmental disorder–not otherwise specified (PDD-NOS). Varying in severity and intensity, common core symptoms include pervasive impairments in the development of reciprocal social interaction and of verbal or nonverbal communication and the presence of restricted, repetitive, and stereotyped patterns of behavior, interest, and activities.

These subtypes of autism can be distinguished from one another in a number of ways. For the diagnosis of autistic disorder (classic autism or Kanner's), all the core features must be present with evidence of significant delays in early language and intelligence. Asperger's disorder (also known as Asperger syndrome) differs from classic autism in that there are no clinically significant delays in language or intelligence. Rett's Disorder is a rare condition diagnosed only in females that includes a characteristic pattern of diminished head growth, loss of purposeful hand skills, and poorly coordinated motor movements. Children with childhood disintegrative disorder regress in core areas after developing normally in the first 2 years of life. PDD-NOS is used as a diagnostic category when criteria are not met for a specific pervasive developmental disorder.

CHARACTERISTICS

Since people with autism are as different from one another as are any other people, characteristic problems in socialization, communication, and imagination manifest in a range of unique ways. The well-known neurologist Oliver Sacks (1995) writes of the difficulty of providing an accurate description of autism in his book *An Anthropologist on Mars*:

> No two people with autism are the same; its precise form or expression is different in every case. Moreover, there may be a most intricate (and potentially creative) interaction between the autistic traits and the other qualities of the individual. So, while a single glance may suffice for clinical diagnosis, if we hope to understand the autistic individual, nothing less than a total biography will do. (p. 250)

Research emanating from a variety of disciplines allows us to construct a picture of autism that draws on clinical and naturalistic observations. When this picture is viewed as a whole, we can begin to piece together a somewhat consistent portrait of how an individual with autism might experience life differently from "neurotypicals" (a term that my friends with Asperger's and high-functioning autism assign to people who present typical neurological profiles).

Social Relatedness

The classic picture of "autistic aloneness" is most evident in early development. Hallmarks of autism include qualitative impairments in social interaction as manifested in a number of distinct ways (American Psychiatric Association, 2000). Children with autism show impaired use of nonverbal behaviors (such as eye gaze, facial expression, body postures, and gestures) in relating socially to others. While able to imitate in mechanical ways (for instance, echoing what someone says, copying motor actions) they show impaired capacities in social imitation (Rogers & Williams, 2006). There is a paucity of seeking out others to share enjoyment or interests. Socioemotional reciprocity or intersubjectivity is therefore lacking (Hobson, 2005). They further face notable challenges in forming peer relationships appropriate to their developmental level.

Wing and Gould (1979) describe three distinct qualities of social behavior that characterize children with autism. *Aloof* children appear to be totally withdrawn and unresponsive to others' social gestures and speech. They may give the impression of avoiding eye contact and physical touch. They may approach others to fulfill simple wants and needs but seem to treat people as if they are inanimate objects. They do not show joint attention, such as using eye gaze or gesture to attract another person's attention to the same object, person, or event for the purpose of sharing an interest.

Passive children appear indifferent to others and may be easily led into social situations. They are generally compliant and willingly go along with others when others take the initiative in making social contact. They may have good speech and respond to clear and simply put questions. They are unresponsive in many of the same ways as "aloof" children in their lack of joint attention with others. They seem unable to communicate their intentions through facial expressions and gestures, as well as unable to interpret others' intentions by reading facial cues.

Active-odd children enjoy being with other people, particularly adults. They may approach people to interact, but they do so in an awkward or idiosyncratic manner. For example, they might go up to and touch a total stranger. They may attempt to carry on a one-sided conversation relating to an obsessive interest that is of little interest to others. Like both "aloof" and "passive" children, they lack the social perceptiveness necessary for communicating effectively and establishing social relations.

Communication and Language

Children with autism display a range of problems in communication and language that are closely tied to social difficulties (Tager-Flusberg, Paul,

& Lord, 2005). In terms of verbal communication, a number of children with autism fail to develop speech. They may never produce words that are recognizable and thus remain functionally mute. Some children develop speech early in development but appear to lose this capacity. Others who virtually never speak may on occasion unexpectedly utter a word or phrase. In some cases, individuals may obtain access to alternative augmentative communication systems such as sign language, pictographic/written symbol systems, or computer-assisted devices with varying degrees of success (Mirenda, 2003).

Children with autism who develop the capacity for speech exhibit a number of unusual features. Echolalia, pronoun reversals, "metaphorical language," and neologisms are among the peculiarities of language in autism. Echolalia is an especially common phenomenon in which children repeat words and phrases they have heard, either immediately or at some time later. Echolalia may be either communicative or noncommunicative in terms of its functionality. Some clinicians suggest that echolalic utterances offer a foundation on which to obtain access to and build more spontaneous and diverse language (Schuler, 2003; Schuler & Fletcher, 2002).

Pronoun reversals, involving the substitution of *I* and *me* for *you* and vice versa, are also common in autism. Similarly, many children refer to themselves in the third person. This may partially relate to the predilection toward echolalia, in which children naturally use pronouns they hear spoken by another person. For instance, the child might parrot a part of the question "Do you want a cookie?" with "You want a cookie" to indicate affirmation. Another explanation may be that children with autism confuse the roles of listener and speaker because of a fundamental problem in integrating relevant information (Frith, 2003).

"Metaphorical language," a term introduced by Kanner, refers to the child's use of idiosyncratic remarks to express a desire or reaction to a certain event. These expressions are not actually metaphoric in nature, but rather involve unique associations understood by the child with autism and others who are aware of that child's personal experience in creating that association (Frith, 2003). A child might associate a phrase from a story book or nursery rhyme with a particular event; for example, the child might repeat the phrase "the old man is snoring" when it rains. Similarly, many children with autism use neologisms—that is, create new words—that have idiosyncratic meaning. For instance, a child I knew invented the word "rolly-rolly" to mean *quesadilla*.

Difficulties in the pragmatics of communication are a universal feature of autism (Baron-Cohen, 1988; Twachtman-Cullen, 2008). Even individuals who develop highly advanced linguistic capabilities experience problems with the rules of conversation appropriate to the social context.

They have problems with nonverbal aspects of communication, such as conveying and comprehending intent with gesture, facial expression, eye gaze, and intonation of voice. Because they are unable to take the listener's perspective, their speech can be circumscribed, lengthy, and pedantic. This relates to a lack of understanding of the nuances and subtle meanings of language expressions such as in the case of idioms. People with autism tend to be excessively literal in their interpretation and use of language.

Patterns of Behavior, Interests, and Activity

Patterns of behavior, interest, and activities that are restricted, repetitive, and stereotyped in nature are a defining feature of autism (American Psychiatric Association, 2000). These unusual behavior patterns coincide with a lack of flexible imagination and highlight the apparent need for order and ritual. They may also relate to sensory-regulation issues (Dunn, 2008). Evident at the time of an autism spectrum diagnosis, these may be manifested in a variety of ways across the age span (Richler, Bishop, Kleinke, & Lord, 2007; South, Ozonoff, & McMahon, 2005).

Children with autism exhibit a range of sensory-oriented behaviors, including stereotyped body movements such as finger waving, arm flapping, and body rocking. Similarly, they may carry out perseverative activity with objects such as repetitively chewing on toys, spinning plates, and flicking light switches. In more severe cases, they may repeatedly engage in self-injurious behavior such as hand biting, head banging, and hair pulling. These simple actions tend to appear in excess as repeated loops of behavior (Frith, 2003).

Elaborate routines involving complex sequences of actions and thoughts are also common in autism. These often appear as rigid and inflexible patterns of activity with self-imposed structure. Children may insist on following a precise routine each day without variation such as always being the third student to enter the school bus, always sitting in the third seat on the bus, and always being the third student to leave the school bus.

Ritualistic behavior can be seen in children's preoccupations with parts of objects, as in organizing objects according to size or taking things apart and putting them back together. Older children and adults may collect things that are of unusual interest, for example, telephone books from cities that start with the letter *B* or the names of all the major law firms in New York City.

I once worked with a child (secretly nicknamed Salvador Dali) whose preoccupation with clocks and calendars were manifested in some unique ways. He frequently approached people to remove their watches from their wrists. For a period of time he threw containers of milk and cups of coffee at a wall clock in the classroom. He later obsessively washed the wall clock with a squeegee after an initial demonstration. He also developed a passion for drawing clocks and calendars denoting times and dates for various events, including keeping track of his classmates' and teachers' birthdays.

Islets of Ability

A number of individuals with autism show remarkable isolated talents or abilities, called "islets of intelligence" by Kanner (Hermelin, 2001; Treffert, 2006). For instance, many children with autism perform exceptionally well on tests involving visual-spatial ability and rote memory skills despite poor performance in other domains. They also may develop hyperlexic or precocious reading skills with little or no instruction. Others show unique aptitude for drawing, music, and calendar calculation. Since Dustin Hoffman's portrayal of an "autistic savant" in the film *Rainman*, rare cases of individuals with autism who have exceptional talents and abilities have gained recognition.

One of the first well-documented cases of extraordinary drawing ability was that of Nadia, a girl who between the ages of 3 and 6 produced some rather remarkable pictures (Selfe, 1977). Nadia had very little language at the time she began drawing. Her drawings resembled the work of a highly talented adolescent artist, showing mastery of visual perspective, fine lines, and vivid action. Inspired by pictures in books, Nadia reproduced her drawings from memory. She drew hundreds of pictures of horses that varied in form and perspective. Nadia gradually produced fewer spontaneous drawings when she began to speak and became more sociable around the age of 7.

Although Nadia possessed an uncanny ability to capture her own visual experience in this isolated form of expression, her drawings were relatively unimaginative and literal in nature. She apparently held images of the details in her mind's eye that enabled her to calculate and graphically represent various visual perspectives. Yet she only represented and manipulated images she saw in pictures. She never attempted to portray an experience, idea, or feeling in her pictures as a way to convey meaning (Gardner, 1982).

A Different Kind of Mind

The notion that we all have "different kinds of minds" is inspired by Mel Levine's (2002) pioneering work in helping parents, professionals, and the children themselves address differences in learning. Recognizing that each individual is unique, most agree that children with autism collectively think and learn differently from their neurotypical counterparts. Explanations for these differences (including influences on variations in play and imagination) have been viewed from diverse theoretical perspectives.

Considerable attention has centered on *theory of mind*—the capacity to recognize and understand that others possess minds or mental states (feeling, desires, intentions, beliefs) that may be the same or different from one's own (Baron-Cohen, 1995; Baron-Cohen, Leslie, & Frith, 1985; Hill & Frith, 2003; Wellman, 1993; Wimmer & Perner, 1983). Precursors to the normal acquisition of a theory of mind begin to emerge in the 1st year of life in the form of joint attention, social imitation, and socioemotional reciprocity, and in the 2nd year of life in the form of symbolic play. Between the ages of 3 and 4, children begin to develop this capacity, which continues to mature until around age 7.

Since children with autism show underlying deficits in all the prerequisite developmental capacities (joint attention, social imitation, socioemotional reciprocity, and symbolic play), it follows that they either fail or experience severe delays in developing a theory of mind. The consequence of having "mindblindness" is far reaching, since interpreting and predicting other people's social behavior is the essence of interpersonal coordination, which is critical to constructing social knowledge.

Other explanations for children with autism having a different kind of mind have also been proposed. *Weak central coherence* is thought to influence how children with autism perceive and ultimately ascribe meaning to objects, people, and events in day-to-day life (Frith, 2003). Research suggests that children with autism show a unique predisposition, and in some cases a heightened capacity, to focus on details (such as parts of objects, single features of a person's face, or isolated elements of a story) while failing to perceive the relationship between these parts in forming a meaningful whole or gestalt (Frith & Happe, 1994). It is quite possible that the young artist Nadia (Selfe, 1977) constructed her paintings by reproducing the minute details she observed, stroke by stroke, without ever perceiving the "big picture." While there are distinct advantages in being able to hone in on and attend to details, as some activities or professions might require (such as identifying coding errors in a computer program), the drawbacks are profound. Most notably, weak central coherence affects the capacity to conceive and comprehend context, especially the richness and meaning that is embedded in language, emotion, and social interaction.

Another explanation that may account for core challenges in autism relates to *executive function* (involving higher-order cognitive skills that include organization, planning, problem solving, self-regulation, and inhibitory control) (Hill, 2004; Hughes, 2001). Researchers speculate that children with autism have *executive dysfunction*, which has been linked to many pervasive features of autism, including repetitiveness, lack of generativity, and inflexible imagination (South, Ozonoff, & McMahon, 2005). Impairment in this area may help to elucidate many of the challenges that people with autism encounter while adapting to and performing in real-life situations. These may include difficulties in initiating and completing tasks and routines, adjusting to changes in the environment, making alternative plans in unexpected situations, and inhibiting responses in social situations (such as making an offensive comment about someone's appearance).

An alternative explanation that is receiving increased attention in the autism literature is the notion of *enactive mind* (Klin, Jones, Schultz, & Volkmar, 2003). Drawing on a larger body of work discussing "embodied mind" (Lakoff & Johnson, 1999), this theory proposes that all aspects of the mind (ideas, thoughts, concepts) are shaped by the body and brain as experienced through perception, movement, and interaction in the environment. In particular, children build mental representations or mental models that are "embodied" in early experiences involving social action with others. This process is thought to be disrupted in the early development of children with autism because of an apparent lack of attunement to salient social stimuli (eye gaze, facial expressions, gestures) and a corresponding focus on irrelevant features in the environment. While selectively attending to a range of physical as opposed to social stimuli, children with autism follow a path of development in which they gain expertise in understanding things rather than people. They develop mental models that reflect a very different view and experience of the social world. Oliver Sacks (1995) related the experience of Temple Grandin, a woman with autism who has remarkable insight into her disorder:

> It has to do . . . with an implicit knowledge of social conventions and codes, of cultural presuppositions of every sort. This implicit knowledge, which every normal person accumulates and generates throughout life on the basis of experience and encounters with others, Temple seems to be largely devoid of. Lacking it, she has instead to "compute" others' feelings and intentions and states of mind, to try to make algorithmic, explicit, what for the rest of us is second nature (p. 270).

SUMMARY

Autism spectrum disorders are variants of a complex neurobiological condition, which typically appears during the first 3 years of life. While the rising rate of autism is partly caused by better identification and changes in diagnostic criteria, hereditary patterns and environmental factors are also suspected. People with autism manifest different symptoms over the life span that may range from mild to severe. Core features of autism include qualitative differences in social relatedness, communication and language, patterns of interest, behavior and activity, islets of ability, and the developing mind. Intricately tied to this unique constellation of features are problems in social and imaginary play. In the following chapter we will look closely at the nature of play to better understand the dilemma it poses for children with autism.

CHAPTER   3

The Nature of Play

I remember as a little girl playing runaway orphans with my two younger sisters and a neighborhood friend. We were quite fond of the popular tales *Peter Pan* and *Oliver Twist*. We gathered together all our dolls and stuffed animals in blankets. My one sister brought along Mr. Peabody, her imaginary friend. Together we set out to explore the "never-never land" of all the backyards in the neighborhood. Every step of the way we encountered a new adventure—imagining near escapes from evil foes, seeking refuge in forts of leaves and snow.

IT IS DIFFICULT to picture my childhood void of the pleasurable images and sensations I associate with play. I had a rich play life typical of my peer culture with special playmates; favorite playthings; secret places; and sweet, precious time in which to explore, create, and imagine. I wondered about children with autism who do not experience play in the same way as typically developing children. What might they be missing by not playing? Why is play so important in children's lives? This chapter explores the nature of play from a variety of theoretical perspectives.

PLAY AS A UNIVERSAL PHENOMENON

Certainly children have played since the beginning of time. Archaeological findings show that almost every culture provided toys for play throughout history. As early as the classical period in Western civilization, humans have struggled to understand play and its meaning for society. While debates abound concerning the functions and value of play, the fact remains that play exists and is ubiquitous in childhood.

Research shows that play is evident across all cultures, ethnic groups, and socioeconomic strata, among children raised alone and with siblings, in urban and rural settings, and under healthy and unhealthy conditions (Pelligrini & Smith, 2005; Schwartzman, 1978; Singer & Singer, 1990). While play, like all aspects of childhood, has transformed over the centuries in light of social, cultural, and environmental factors, the drive to play is unequivocal. Under less than optimal conditions, and even in the face of adversity, the child's impulse to play endures.

Children growing up under diverse circumstances, including of social and economic oppression, have documented histories of highly imaginative games and toys (Chudacoff, 2007). For instance, children of African descent who grew up as slaves on plantations in the southern United States had an immensely rich play culture that continues to inspire children's play today (Smith, 1963). Appalachia, an area that historically has been largely economically deprived, has an elaborate collection of creative games and toys passed on from generation to generation (Page & Smith, 1985).

Portraits of children playing among the shadows and devastation of war attest to play's impelling force. George Eisen (1988) provides an especially graphic historical portrait of children's play during the Holocaust:

> A special place must be devoted to the existence of children's play, though unwitting, during the final stages of the extermination process. Indeed, play burst forth spontaneously and uncontrollably without regard to the external situation. Children on their way to the gas chambers were not always aware what awaited them at the end of the dusty road. Yet even amidst the surrealistic landscape of death, in the extermination centers, the fluttering presence of rare moments of a child forgetting or ignoring the ever-present death is real. Among the many painful scenes, there were unique instances when the prisoners, and sometimes even their executioners, stood with tears in their eyes watching a playing child entering the gas chamber. Children spent their precious last moments in play. (p. 66)

Whether play surfaces in response to biological, environmental, or a combination of factors, one must appreciate its existence as the very fabric of childhood culture—a powerful force that stands the test of human existence. These robust and thriving qualities compel us to look deeper at play and seriously consider its striking absence in children with autism.

CHARACTERISTICS OF PLAY

While criteria for deciding whether or not a child is playing may seem obvious, defining play is notoriously complex. In part because of the various disciplines involved in investigating play and the different approaches they take in analyzing different aspects of play, there is little consensus on a precise definition (Sutton-Smith, 2001). Anthropology, philosophy, sociology, psychology, and education greatly vary in the motives and methodologies employed to study play. Most researchers have recognized that different types of play may need to be defined in different ways and that definitions are likely to vary according to one's theoretical biases (Smith, Takhvar, Gore, & Vollstedt, 1986).

Among those best known for their study of play, there is general agreement on some of the characteristics that distinguish play from nonplay behavior (Garvey, 1977; Rubin, Fein, & Vandenberg, 1983; Smith & Vollstedt, 1985). The following characteristics of play are evident among typically developing children everywhere:

- *Play is pleasurable.* Children's delight in play is commonly accompanied by signs of positive affect. Although not essential, smiling and laughter are often signs of a playful orientation. Children engaged in playful activities may also exhibit other signs, such as blissful humming or singing to themselves.
- *Play requires active engagement.* Children become deeply absorbed in play activities as they explore, experiment, and create. This may be differentiated from inactive or passive states, such as aimless wandering or lounging. In some cases, daydreaming—when children play with ideas or invent fantasy—reflects active engagement.
- *Play is voluntary and intrinsically motivated.* In play, children freely choose the activity. The motivation to play comes from within the child, occurring without external demands or rewards. The goals of play are self-imposed rather than imposed by others.
- *Play involves attention to means over ends.* In play, there is greater attention on the process than on the attainment of a particular goal or outcome. Implicit goals within play are flexible, self-imposed, and continually redefined within the context of the activity. There is an open-ended quality that differentiates play from goal-directed activities, such as work and organized games with a predetermined set of rules.
- *Play is flexible and changing.* In play, children are free to do the unexpected, change the rules, and experiment with novel combinations of behavior and ideas. Play is forever being transformed as children vary, elaborate, and diversify existing themes and repertoires. This quality of play stands in contrast to highly rigid and perseverative behavior characteristic of stereotyped activity.

- *Play has a nonliteral orientation.* This characteristic distinguishes play from nonplay behavior as children treat objects, actions, or events "as if" they were something else. This is evident when a child transforms an object in pretend play; a broom is not used for sweeping, but is used as if it were a horse. A nonliteral orientation is also apparent when children simulate realistic actions or events; the children are not really fighting, but are play fighting.

INFLUENTIAL THEORIES OF PLAY

Romantic Theories

Jean-Jacques Rousseau's popular philosophical writings in eighteenth-century Europe brought forth a new consciousness of childhood that laid the foundation for current conceptions of play in the education and treatment of children. He regarded play as natural childhood activity characterized by qualities of curiosity and joyfulness. In his didactic novel *Émile*, he wrote of the young child: "Work or play are all one for him, his games are his work; he knows no difference. He brings to everything the cheerfulness of his interest, the charm of freedom, and he shows the bent of his own mind and the extent of his knowledge" (1762/1956, p. 26). He furthermore suggested building on the child's natural interests and proclivities in play as a means to gradually develop his or her potential.

Around the same period, Jean-Marc-Gaspard Itard, a pioneer in special education, applied similar notions of play in his work with Victor, who came to be known as the "wild boy of Aveyron" (Lane, 1979). This feral child appeared to be about 12 years of age when he was discovered wandering in a forest in central France. There is now strong evidence to suggest that he actually had autism. Taking on the challenge of educating Victor in his home, Itard adopted an approach that involved tailoring instruction based on the behavior, interests, and needs of his pupil. As a part of this process, Itard submitted to giving himself over to Victor's unusual fascinations: "People may say what they like, but I confess that I lend myself without ceremony to all this childish play" (quoted in Lane, 1979, p. 95).

Classical Theories

Classical theories emerged to explain the existence of children's play and its purpose in development (Ellis, 1973). The surplus-energy theory can be traced back to the German poet Friedrich Schiller (1759–1805) and the British philosopher Herbert Spencer (1820–1903). According to this theory, children let out their excess energy—energy that would otherwise be necessary for daily survival activities—in play. Schiller further speculated that play, being a luxury, served to establish a sense of "aesthetic" appreciation in humankind. This initiated the view of play as a medium through which the player transforms and transcends reality, thereby gaining new symbolic representations of the world.

Philosopher Karl Groos's (1901) practice theory contended that play strengthens instincts vital for adaptation and survival of the species. In this view, childhood is a period in which to practice and perfect skills necessary for adulthood. He noted children's concern for the process of play rather than the attainment of a product. Groos described different stages and types of play, each serving an adaptive function in interpersonal and intrapersonal development.

Child Study and Progressive Movements

The child study movement flourished under the influence of G. Stanley Hall (1906), who propelled interest in scientific research methods to observe and collect data on children's behavior and development. Hall extended Darwinian perspectives on evolution to the recapitulation theory of play. According to this theory, children reenact the developmental stages of the human race in their play. He suggested that play is linked to innate patterns of behavior serving to rid children of primitive instincts before going on to the realities of adult life. Although Hall's research methods were questioned by his followers, this theory influenced the view accepted later that play serves a cathartic function.

John Dewey (1902) and followers of the Progressive movement in education sought to base curriculum on pragmatics, emphasizing the notion that the child's own experience forms the basis for discovery and learning. He encouraged a playful orientation in the process of acquiring knowledge through exploration, inquiry, problem solving, and creativity. Dewey also stressed the importance of social learning, in which playing with others serves to prepare children as citizens of a democratic society. Dewey's notions of play exerted tremendous influence on the evolution of early childhood education.

Psychoanalytic Theories

Sigmund Freud (1920/1961) and followers of his psychoanalytic theory offered an interpretation of play that had a significant impact on the treatment of childhood disorders. From the psychoanalytic viewpoint, play is the projection of the child's inner or emotional life. Accordingly, play acts serve to satisfy drives, resolve inner conflicts, and help a child cope with anxiety-producing situations. Thus play's role was considered to be primarily a therapeutic one, serving to prevent and cure emotional problems.

Extending Freud's theory, Erik Erikson (1950) postulated that play serves as an "ego function" independent of the child's need to resolve conflicts. According to his theory, play progresses through stages that mirror children's psychosocial development. Children create model situations in play that help them cope with the demands of reality. In particular, they learn to master emotions and frustrations through repetition and reconstruction of painful or frightening events. Considering play to be important to children's intellectual, emotional, and social development, Susan Isaacs (1933) interpreted this view for teachers in her work in early childhood education.

Constructivist Theories

Cognitive theorists Jean Piaget (1962) and Lev Vygotsky (1966, 1978) viewed play in a broader context, giving it central importance in children's intellectual development. Both Piaget and Vygotsky recognized play as a manifestation of the child's developing semiotic function. The acquisition of higher-level cognitive abilities occurs as a gradual process through the transformation of objects, roles, and situations in play. From a Piagetian perspective, play is self-initiated activity that forms the basis for acquiring distinct ways of thinking and behaving. Children are intrinsically motivated to play because they derive satisfaction from the activity and from mastery over objects and events. On the basis of this assumption, play development is a solo journey with all sources of change manifested within the child.

Sociocultural Theories

Unlike Piaget, Vygotsky conceptualized play as social activity in which children construct shared meanings and transform their understanding of the skills, values, and knowledge inherent to their culture. Even solitary play is considered social activity, since the themes, roles, and scripts enacted in play represent the child's understanding and appropriation of the sociocultural materials of society. This notion of play conforms to the main premise of Vygotsky's psychological theory, which is that the transmission of culture through social interaction is critical to the formation of mind.

Social activity is essentially the driving force in the development of higher psychological processes, with all higher functions originating in relations between humans. According to Vygotsky, play creates the "zone of proximal development" in which individual development occurs during joint problem solving with people who have skill in the use of cultural tools. He defined the "zone of proximal development" as

> the distance between the child's actual developmental level as determined by independent problem solving and the level of potential development as determined through problem solving under adult guidance or in collaboration with more capable peers. (1978, p. 86)

Vygotsky believed that play is significant not only in reflecting development, but also in leading development:

> In play a child always behaves beyond his average age, above his daily behavior; in play it is as though he were a head taller than himself. As in the focus of a magnifying glass, play contains all developmental tendencies in a condensed form and is itself a major source of development. (p. 102)

Commensurate with a Vygotskian perspective is the notion that since children regard play as the most highly valued social activity, it is the very essence of peer culture (Corsaro, 2005; Wolfberg et al., 1999). *Play culture* more precisely depicts that realm in which children together create social and imaginary worlds (Mouritsen, 1996; Selmer-Olson, 1993). One important aspect of play culture is that children form a sense of collective identity in which they regard themselves as belonging to a group created by and for children to the exclusion of adults. Although adult cultural activities and products may be represented within the content of the play culture, children carry out play on their own terms, in spite of adult expectations (see, for example, Powell, 2007). Another aspect of play culture is that play is children's living folklore, something children produce and pass on between themselves. From this perspective, play is based on children's participation in culturally defined activities that steadily change and develop with new conditions of society. Thus play culture applies to children of all ages and manifests itself in children's jokes, riddles, rhymes, songs, narratives, writings, drawings, creations, imaginings, collections, and rituals. Moreover, skill and practice are a part of the tradition passed on in children's play culture.

PLAY'S SIGNIFICANCE IN CHILDHOOD

Tracing influential theories from past to present, we can appreciate play's social, cultural, and developmental significance in childhood. A growing body of evidence that supports play's associations with attainments in cognition, social competence, language and literacy, artistic expression, and emotional development speak to the importance of play (Elkind, 2007; Fromberg & Bergen, 2006; Isenberg & Quisenberry, 2002; Singer, Golinkoff, & Hirsh-Pasek, 2006).

Play and Cognition

Play's relationship to children's cognition is one of the most researched areas in the play literature. Children's growing awareness of the function and meaning of objects develops through exploring and manipulating objects in play (Fenson & Schell, 1986). Knowledge of functional, spatial, causal, and categorical relationships derives from early play activities. In pretend play, children can think about meanings without being constrained by the physical properties of an object or the reality of a situation. They are able to conceive of objects and situations as representing other objects and situations. This increasing capacity to transform objects and manipulate symbols in pretend play ties to the development of association, logical memory, and abstract thought (Piaget, 1962; Vygotsky, 1966, 1978).

Play generates flexibility and creativity in behavior and thinking, allowing for efficient and innovative solutions to problems (Sutton-Smith, 1967; Sylva, Bruner, & Genova, 1976). When provided with opportunities to explore and create, children will experiment with new and unusual combinations of behavior that might not occur in externally structured situations. In pretend play, children can break free from conventional mental associations and put ideas together in novel and flexible ways. Play experiences therefore result in an enlarged collection of creative ideas and associations.

Play and Social Competence

A major contribution of play is its influence on children's social competence. Peer play is an especially important social and cultural context within which children acquire various skills equated with social competence (Corsaro, 2005; Kupfersmidt & Dodge, 2004; Ladd, 2005). While engaged in joint activity, children refine increasingly complex and sophisticated social communication strategies (Rubin & Thompson, 2003). For instance, they learn to express and interpret subtle social cues to successfully extend invitations and gain entry into peer group activities. They also learn to negotiate and compromise to resolve conflicts over space, materials, and play roles. Peer play further provides children opportunities to express intimacy and affection, which are core ingredients of friendship (Dunn, 2004).

Pretend play has special significance for children's social development (Fromberg & Bergen, 2006). Since aspects of the social world and expectations about the behavior of people provide the main materials for social pretend play, while collaborating on play scripts children test out hypotheses about possible interactions and relationships among humans (Howes et al., 1992). In social pretend play, children also construct a shared understanding of literal and nonliteral meaning while mastering social communication (Bretherton, 1984; Garvey, 1977).

Play, Language, and Literacy

Play's implicit relationship to language and literacy is supported by a large body of research (Zigler, Singer, & Bishop-Josef, 2004). In early development, children play with different forms and rules of language (Bruner, 1990; Weir, 1976). Through experimentation with phonological, syntactic, and semantic rules, they practice and perfect newly acquired language skills and develop metalinguistic awareness (Cazden, 1976). This relates to the increasing capacity to represent objects, actions, and feelings in play as established through language (McCune-Nicholich, 1981, Nicholich, 1977).

This shift from playful action to linguistic play represents the discovery and realization of narrative structures, which later give rise to literary imagination (Gardner, 1982). Narrative competence and story comprehension relate to children's reconstruction of narrative scripts in symbolic play, involving the abstraction of characters' actions, goals, and language from life experiences (Nicolopoulou, McDowell, & Brockmeyer, 2006; Pellegrini, 1985).

Peer play is an especially important context enabling children to learn new vocabulary, complex language structures (Ervin-Tripp, 1991), and the rules of conversation (Garvey, 1977). Dyson (1991) documented the roots of children's language and literacy development in case illustrations of schoolchildren's jointly constructed dramatic play scripts.

Play and Artistic Expression

The early childhood years represent the "golden age of creativity," when inventiveness and imagination are unleashed not only in children's play but also in artistic expression through different forms of media (Gardner, 1982). The complex and intricate process of symbolization in play parallels that of symbolization in different forms of creative expression (Vygotsky, 1978). Dyson (1991) illustrated the intricate relationship between play, spoken language, writing, and drawing, documenting the gradual fusion with imagination as children collaborated in playful activity.

Just as they do in play, children express themselves individually when they approach and explore a range of art media (such as drawing and painting). For some children, drawings are "windows on an engaging play world," while for others drawing is a catalyst for dramatic play (Gardner, Wolf, & Smith, 1982). Expressions in drawing through line, shape, and form often convey feelings, experiences, and stories in ways that are similar to the child's effort to make sense of the world through play (Coles, 1992).

Play and Emotional Development

Play has long been acknowledged as serving an important role in children's emotional development. According to Elkind (1981), "Play is nature's way of dealing with stress for children as well as adults" (p. 197). An enduring theory is that play has a cathartic effect by allowing children to work through and master perplexing and traumatic experiences of the past and present (Axline, 1947; Erikson, 1950; Freud, 1961). Dramatization of fears and anxieties enables children to better understand themselves and gain a sense of control over external events in their lives. For instance, I observed a 7-year-old girl retell the tragic events of the Twin Towers being destroyed on September 11, 2001, while pretending to be a television news reporter with a group of peers. She poignantly ended her news report with the statement, "Now back to the sunshine."

There is also evidence to suggest that social pretend play is linked to self-regulation in childhood (Berk, Mann, & Ogan, 2006). Self-regulation reflects the child's increasing capacity to exert self-control over emotions; resist impulses; and guide his or her own thoughts, actions, and behaviors in a socially accepted manner. Thus, imaginative play, especially with peers, provides a firm foundation for children's social and emotional growth.

SUMMARY

Play is a universal phenomenon evident among children from all walks of life. Children strive to play even under the most devastating conditions. This causes special concern for children with autism who experience problems in play even in the best of circumstances. There are many ways in which to define play, each offering a different means for observing and interpreting children's behavior. The working definition proposed here includes descriptive features that distinguish play from nonplay behavior. A number of influential theories helped to shape contemporary conceptions of play. Current research connects play to childhood culture and development in multiple ways. In light of its social, cultural, and developmental significance, play deserves consideration as a meaningful instructional context and social activity. In the following chapter we look more closely at the role of play in development, comparing typical childhood experiences with those of children with autism.

CHAPTER 4

Play in Childhood Development

There was a child went forth every day,
And the first object he look'd upon, that object
    he became;
And that object became part of him for the day,
    or a certain part of the day,
Or for many years or stretching cycles of years.
The early lilacs became part of this child,
And grass and white and red morning glories,
    and white and red clover, and the song of
    the phoebe-bird,
And the Third-month lambs and the sow's pink-
    faint litter, and the mare's foal and the cow's
    calf.
                              —Walt Whitman, *Leaves of grass*

WALT WHITMAN'S PERCEPTION of childhood captures the essence of play most children experience throughout their development. Venturing into the world with natural curiosity and delight, the child becomes one with the sights, sounds, and textures of life encountered each day. Play emerges and transforms as children make connections with physical objects and social beings in an ever-widening web of cultural experience. When do children first begin to play? What happens to play as children grow older? How does the play of children with autism differ from that of typically developing children? This chapter follows the course of symbolic and social play in typical childhood development, providing a context for understanding play variations in children with autism.

PLAY'S NATURAL COURSE IN CHILDHOOD

While play's natural course in typical childhood follows a relatively consistent progression, each child's path varies in light of sociocultural, biological, and environmental influences (Fromberg & Bergen, 2006). Moreover, it is important to recognize that the development of play does not proceed along a linear path in an unambiguous, stage-by-stage fashion. Rather, various forms of play emerge out of a confluence of intricately woven developmental attainments that surface and peak at various points across the age span.

Roots of Play

It is not easy to ascertain when children first begin to play. Nevertheless, playful behavior is evident during the first few months of life, when infants exchange gazes and take turns vocalizing with caregivers (Garvey, 1977). Even infants as young as 8 weeks of age display signs of a playful orientation as they vigorously smile and coo when interacting with people, as well as with objects that provide contingent responses (such as a mobile controlled by a string tied to the baby's leg) (Watson, 1976). Play experiences involving joint attention and contingent responding reflect the highly transactional nature of play.

Playful interactions between adult caregivers and infants in their 1st year of life appear to be the earliest form of social play. In the first 6 months, infants mainly play an appreciative role in social games initiated by adults, such as peekaboo and pat-a-cake (Ross & Kay, 1980). Adults engage the infant by performing a sequence of actions contingent on the infant's response (Stern, 1974). To elicit such responses as smiling, laughter, and eye gaze, adults engage the infant with exaggerated and varied facial expressions, vocalizations, and tactile contacts.

Infants increasingly take an active role in social play as they develop. While laughing and smiling in anticipation of the actions performed by adults, they begin to discover rhythm in the give-and-take of social games. Initially they take turns in a hesitant manner, relying on adult responses to carry out the sequence. To encourage greater participation, the adult regulates the amount of support provided in relation to the child's advancing ability to initiate and sustain social play exchanges (Bruner & Sherwood, 1976). Eventually the infant takes confident and regular turns and initiates familiar play sequences.

Social play directed toward peers also follows a relatively consistent sequence in early development (Hartup, 1983; Hay, Payne, & Chadwick, 2004). Infants begin to actively express interest in peers at around 6 months of age. They direct natural signs toward peers by looking, smiling, vocalizing, gesturing, and reaching out and touching them. They also show that they recognize familiar peers by responding to them in idiosyncratic ways. A period follows in which infants engage in brief and fleeting encounters with peers by offering and exchanging toys, mutually manipulating objects, and occasionally imitating toy play.

In early development, play with objects progresses from repetitious and undifferentiated actions to predictable and organized play sequences. Initially infants actively explore by mouthing, reaching, and banging various objects. Attending to single objects, they apply appropriate action schemes such as pulling, twisting, or turning knobs. They subsequently combine and use objects as containers to explore relational properties. Eventually, they recognize and use familiar objects in conventional ways, such as drinking from a cup or combing hair.

Physical objects in the immediate environment often become vehicles for social play exchanges (Garvey, 1977). At approximately 9 months of age, infants display the capacity to coordinate attention between people and objects. Although not yet able to talk, they use intentional communication to attract attention by vocalizing, gesturing, showing, or giving objects. They actively seek out others to obtain an object out of reach or to demonstrate how to manipulate the object correctly.

It is during this period that infants develop joint attention involving an active process of shared attention on an object or event. At the same time they learn to respond to the emotional cues of adults, a capacity known as social referencing (Sorce & Emde, 1981). An adult's emotional reaction to a particular object or event directly affects the infant's exploration of that object or event. For example, babies will hesitate to carry out an action—such as leaving a particular area or picking up an object about which an adult expresses alarm or distaste. This period of development reflects the early capacity to form representations of people, things, and events.

Joint attention and social referencing are significant as an entry point not only for the child's understanding that a given object or event can have meaning for self and others, but also for an appreciation of the multiple-meanings nature of symbolism (Hobson, 2005). Sophisticated forms of symbolic activity, including pretend play, are thus rooted in the infant's experience of a world of shared feelings and patterns of activity with others. This has profound implications for children with autism, whose lack of joint attention is often one of the earliest signs of the condition.

Play in Early Childhood

Singer and Singer (1990) refer to early childhood as the "high season of imaginative play" (p. 64). As children make the transition to this period, a number of related capacities emerge, reflecting the reorganization of thought. Following a similar progression, symbolic play develops along several dimensions (Garvey, 1977; Nicholich, 1977; Rubin et al., 1983;

Westby, 2000). Children gradually incorporate primitive symbolic representations into play sequences with objects and people. Governed by internal representations of ideas, rules, or symbols, they assign new and novel meanings to objects. They increasingly use props in abstract and inventive ways in which an object stands for something else or something totally imaginary is created. Thematic content in play reflects the increasing use of gestures and language to invent novel, elaborate, and integrated play scripts. Children organize imaginative play themes with greater coherence and complexity. They eventually adopt roles in play and treat inanimate objects (such as dolls and stuffed animals) as if they could initiate their own actions.

At this particular juncture in play development, children with autism experience the greatest difficulty. Here it is important to make a distinction between two forms of play. *Functional play* (also referred to as *relational play, reality-oriented play,* or *simple pretense*) emerges around 18 months of age. In this type of play, children respond to an object's actual properties (Harris, 1989). They demonstrate the appropriate use of an object or the conventional association of two or more objects (Ungerer & Sigman, 1981). They initially rely on realistic props to reenact brief and isolated actions directed to objects (pushing a car on the floor or placing a cup on a saucer) and familiar routines directed at themselves (holding a cup to their mouth). They later reenact the isolated actions of others and extend simple play scripts to dolls and other people (holding a cup to a doll's mouth).

Symbolic pretend play (also referred to as *make-believe, imaginary play,* and *advanced pretense*) emerges between 2 and 3 years of age. The transition from functional to symbolic pretend play signifies the child's emerging capacity to form representations of representations, or metarepresentations. In this type of play, the child is able to disengage from reality and entertain nontruths. Leslie (1987) proposed three fundamental forms of symbolic play: (1) object substitution, that is, using one object to represent another (pretending a banana is a telephone), (2) attribution of absent or false properties (pretending that a dry table is wet), and (3) imaginary objects as present (pretending that an empty cup contains tea).

Children initially organize play scripts around familiar events they have personally experienced. They intentionally incorporate the necessary lifelike props appropriate for the activity into play scripts. Such a script might include putting a doll to bed with its pajamas, a blanket, and pillow, and commenting, "Baby sleeping." Play scripts later incorporate themes around familiar events performed by others, such as grocery shopping with a doll. At this stage children begin to talk to dolls ("Baby go shopping") but do not yet project their feelings or desires on to dolls.

Between 3 and 4 years of age, children rely less on realistic replicas or lifelike props to pretend and increasingly use language to narrate and plan play scripts. They display the capacity to transform objects, such as using a block to represent a car. They are also able to transform themselves into different play roles by animating toys and dramatizing characters. Moreover, a significant number of children invent imaginary companions, which many maintain for years (Taylor, Carlson, Maring, Gerow, & Charlie, 2004). Eventually, children show the capacity to engage in reciprocal roles in play by taking the part of two or more actors (pretending to be both mother and baby with a doll). By integrating several play scripts, children may engage in elaborate dramas with sequential and evolving play episodes.

The transition from functional to symbolic pretend play signifies a major turning point in the development of children with autism. Pretend play underscores the child's growing capacity to conjure up and infer mental states in others. Imagination is key to forming suppositions about what another might feel, believe, and desire.

With growing exposure to peers, the capacity to coordinate social play dominates the early childhood years. Children cycle back and forth along a continuum that reflects increasing complexity and cohesiveness in social play (Howes et al., 1992; Parten, 1932). Although children prefer the company of peers (Rubin & Thompson, 2003), on occasion they choose *solitary* play (not to be confused with "isolate" play observed in children with autism). Solitary play is seen as a natural extension of social play, since it allows children to practice and appropriate newly acquired skills. Many children spend time observing peers as *onlookers* prior to joining them in play. This helps to orient children to their playmates and activities as well as the social rules, roles, and patterns of the play culture. Playing in *parallel* with similar materials or in the same place alongside peers is a consistent pattern in early childhood development. This type of play stimulates imitation and modeling of observed behaviors. Establishing a *common focus* in play involves reciprocal exchanges that gradually increase in length, frequency, and complexity. The capacity to cooperate or play with a *common goal* next emerges. This type of play is geared to making a product, dramatizing an event, or carrying out a formal game through a collaborative process. This period of development coincides with the ability to coordinate a social pretend framework with peers (McCune-Nicholich, 1981).

Social pretend play requires working together to maintain intersubjectivity while collaborating on play scenarios (Bretherton, 1984; Howes et al., 1992). Themes and dramatic roles are inspired by familiar people, events, and characters as well as pure invention and fantasy. As children mature, they use increasingly flexible, complex, and sophisticated language in social pretend play. Established during the course of play, rules become much more involved.

Play in Middle Childhood

Relatively little attention has been given to the study of play development in later years because of societal constraints and expectations placed upon children as they enter school (Elkind, 2007; Isenberg & Quisenberry, 2002; Singer et al., 2006). A prevalent view is that older children are thought to abandon make-believe play for more advanced play endeavors (Piaget, 1962). Consequently, the limited play activities formally available to children in school generally do not include occasions for pretend. Organized sports and games with highly structured rules typically dominate free-play activities in those schools that offer recess and breaks from academic instruction. While older children undoubtedly find some enjoyment in these highly predictable activities, when they are provided with opportunities for open-ended play the impulse to pretend endures (Fromberg & Bergen, 2006). Further, in cases where the peer culture is deprived of or discouraged from engaging in imaginative play, children have been known to defy adult expectations by covertly seeking it out on their own (Powell, 2007).

There are qualitative differences in the style and content of older children's pretend play as compared with that of younger children. Overt play appears to gradually and subtly transform into private thought or fantasy (Singer & Singer, 1990, 2006). Children pursue their fantasies by seeking out playful activities in different ways. Many children engage in dramatic play with peers, dolls, and miniatures. Some children create elaborately detailed imaginary worlds, or paracosms, that may continue well into adolescence (Cohen & MacKeith, 1991). The complex imagery produced in other representational activities, such as art, writing, and storytelling, also reveal children's fantasies. Older children's play scripts and creative expressions often reflect greater complexity and sophistication than those of younger children; however, they are frequently constrained by concerns for convention and peer acceptance (Gardner, 1989).

Interactive digital media, especially video and computer games, have become a prominent part of children's play culture (Kafai, 2006). To a large extent, these activities offer "ready-made" virtual play worlds in which children control and interact with fantasy figures. Such activities may be pursued either as a solitary or social activity. However, technology is also available that offers tools and opportunities for children to be creative and co-construct their own virtual play worlds in imaginative ways. Kafai (2006) notes:

The current reality of interactive technology tends to undervalue the constructive aspects of play in which children have always engaged. However, electronic building blocks and virtual playgrounds are materials and places that should be accepted as wooden blocks, bricks, and sandboxes. (p. 99)

Older children spend increasing amounts of time in peer play away from the watchful eyes of adults (Ladd, 2005). Their focus is more on establishing stable friendships and affiliations with peer groups. While friendship alliances initially form on the basis of shared common interests, they later are defined in terms of mutual liking, closeness, loyalty, taking care of one another, providing assistance, reducing loneliness, and sharing feelings (Rubin & Thompson, 2006; Staub, 1999). Friendships are also formed on the basis of social status. "Cliques" often develop where its members establish a clear hierarchy while considering age, gender, ethnicity, and other social and cultural factors (Meyer et al., 1987).

Coordinating peer-group activities requires a kind of social finesse that is evident among socially competent or popular children as opposed to children who tend to be neglected or rejected by peers (Putallaz, 1983; Putallaz & Gottman, 1981). Socially competent children use sophisticated verbal and nonverbal social communication strategies to enter established peer-group activities. A graceful entrance relies on establishing a shared frame of reference. Socially competent children generally follow a sequence of strategies that reflects an understanding of the group's perspective. They first gradually approach and hover on the periphery of the group, mimic or comment on the activity, progressively move closer, and wait for an invitation or a natural break to enter the group without disrupting the players (Dodge, Schlundt, Schocken, & Delugach, 1983). Since children with autism are frequently neglected and rejected by peers, mastering the skills necessary for peer-group entry is of critical importance.

PLAY VARIATIONS IN CHILDREN WITH AUTISM

The stark play life of children with autism stands in sharp contrast to that of the typically developing child. Within the spectrum of autism, children greatly vary in terms of their social, cognitive, and linguistic capabilities and thus present very different profiles of play development. Despite apparent differences in the rate and progression of play, children with autism bear striking similarities in the overall quality of their play. Spontaneous, diverse, flexible, creative, and interactive qualities commonly associated with play are characteristically lacking.

An apparent failure to merge object- and people-focused lines of development places children with autism at a distinct disadvantage in play as both a social and symbolic endeavor (Wolfberg & Schuler, 2006). As Williams, Costall, and Reddy (1999) clearly articulate:

> Given the evidence that other people play an important role in introducing objects to children . . . an impairment in interpersonal relations should itself lead us to expect corresponding disruption in the autistic child's use of objects. Conversely, an unusual use of objects is likely to manifest itself in disturbances in relating to other people, given the importance of a shared understanding and use of objects in facilitating interaction. (p. 367).

When given the opportunity to play freely, children with autism are likely to pursue repetitive and stereotyped activities in social isolation (Frith, 2003; Wing, Gould, Yeates, & Brierly, 1977; Williams, Reddy, & Costall, 2001). They may reproduce the same play activity for hours on end—and continue to pursue it for months and even years. Once it is established, many children express considerable resistance to a play routine being disrupted.

Clara Claiborne Park (1967) writes in the opening paragraph of her widely acclaimed book, *The Siege: The First Eight Years of an Autistic Child*, about the detached and repetitive nature of her daughter's early play:

> We start with an image—a tiny, golden child on hands and knees, circling round and round a spot on the floor in mysterious, self-absorbed delight. She does not look up, though she is smiling and laughing; she does not call our attention to the mysterious object of her pleasure. She does not see us at all. She and the spot are all there is, and though she is eighteen months old, an age for touching, tasting, pointing, pushing, exploring, she is doing none of these. . . . She does not *want* any objects. Instead, she circles her spot. Or she sits, a long chain in her hand, snaking it up and down, up and down, watching it coil and uncoil, for twenty minutes, half an hour. (p. 3)

In contrast, Jean-Paul Bovee, now an adult, reflects on his play preferences in middle childhood (Donnelly & Bovee, 2003):

> The play that I liked to do was making lists. These lists were of genealogical family trees of kings, dukes, marquises, earls, counts, etc. I enjoyed reading and writing down the lists, though no one, including me, could read the lists because of my poor handwriting. I also liked to look at the World Book Atlas and write down all of the cities in the world with populations of 15,000 and higher. I could spend a whole weekend doing this. . . . I would also watch the drops from the cleaning fluid or raindrops race down the window. I wanted to see which one would make it down first. It was odd, but it was my play since it was fun for me. (pp. 474–475)

Symbolic Dimension of Play

Children on the autism spectrum present distinct profiles of play development along the symbolic dimension. A number of studies provide strong evidence that children with autism have specific impairments in spontaneous symbolic play that may also affect spontaneous functional play (Jarrold, 2003; Jarrold et al., 1996; Libby et al., 1998; Williams, 2003; Williams et al., 2001).

The tendency to manipulate objects in a stereotyped fashion is one of the most commonly cited characteristics of play in autism. When children with autism are compared with children of a similar maturational age, manipulation play is evident in the former at higher rates than either functional or symbolic pretend play (Dominguez, Ziviani, & Rodger, 2006; Libby et al., 1998; Tilton & Ottinger, 1964). While manipulating objects, children with autism produce fewer distinctly different combinations (Tilton & Ottinger, 1964). Stereotyped play routines range from simple acts, such as banging or shaking objects, to more complex acts, such as stacking or lining up objects according to physical attributes (color, size) or category (cans, bottles). Some children perform extraordinary feats of balance and coordination when they manipulate objects in play.

As noted, children with autism are less likely to play spontaneously with toys in a functional manner. A number of children nevertheless display some capacity for functional play as demonstrated through conventional use and association of toys and objects (Jarrold et al., 1996; Williams et al., 2001). Overall, they produce less diverse functional play, fewer different functional play acts, and fewer functional play acts and sequences (especially directed to dolls) than do children of a similar maturational age (Mundy et al., 1986; Sigman & Ungerer, 1984; Williams et al., 2001). Functional play ranges from simple isolated schemes (pushing a toy car along a surface) and combined schemes (pushing a toy car into a garage) to more complex schemes (constructing an intricate network with interconnecting blocks).

Children with autism rarely spontaneously produce symbolic pretend play. When they do show this capacity, the quality of their play differs from that of typical children in some distinct ways. As compared with developmentally matched peers, children with autism exhibit less advanced pretense, such as object substitutions, treating a doll as an active agent, and inventing imaginary entities (Baron-Cohen, 1987; Lewis & Boucher, 1988; Ungerer & Sigman, 1981). They also generate fewer novel play acts while pretending (Charman & Baron-Cohen, 1997; Jarrold et al., 1996).

There is growing evidence to suggest that more able children on the autism spectrum are capable of engaging in advanced forms of pretend play when it is elicited in structured contexts (Boucher & Lewis, 1990; Charman & Baron-Cohen, 1997; Jarrold et al., 1996; Lewis & Boucher, 1988; Mundy et al., 1986; Riguet et al., 1981; Sigman & Ungerer, 1984). However, pretend play scripts have been observed to be less integrated, varied, and flexible as compared with the play of typically developing children (Harris, 1993). In particular, children with autism have difficulty spontaneously generating and imposing pretend creations on a given context. Even elaborate play scenarios represent well-rehearsed scripts that are prompted by a predictable situation or context. Harris (1993) provides an insightful example:

> D. is an autistic child aged 8 years. . . . One of her favourite routines is pre-tending to be a waitress. At mealtimes, she goes around the family circle asking each member what he or she would like to drink. Having received an order, she briefly mimes writing it down, or tells her customer that it is not available. The circle completed, she leaves the table to get the order. This role-play remains repetitive and fragile. First she repeats the pretend script often; second the repetition rarely incorporates new variations—the same drinks are typically available at the same prices; third, the pretence is not sustained—her customers are lucky to get the drink they ordered, or any drink at all. Once D. has left the table, the script often collapses unless there is further prompting from her customers. (p. 237)

Social Dimension of Play

Children with autism similarly experience pervasive challenges in the development of spontaneous social play. Severe and persistent deficits in joint attention, social imitation and socioemotional reciprocity clearly af-fect the child's capacity to socialize in general (Dissanayake et al., 1996; Sigman & Ruskin, 1999), particularly within the context of play with peers (Jordan, 2003).

Since the nature of social abnormalities in autism tends to change with age, with the most severe global problems manifesting in early develop-ment, specific problems in peer relations are difficult to discern during this period (Howlin, 1986; Rutter, 1978). Social isolation, nevertheless, marks this early period of development with peer interactions adversely affected (Frith, 2003).

Many children with autism, particularly more able children, show noticeable improvements in socialization after the age of 5; however, so-cial abnormalities that do persist clearly affect peer play (Lord, 1984). The extent to which children with autism are socially responsive to others in play is contingent upon such factors as severity and quality of the social impairment, familiarity, and experience with specific peers and play events, and the structure of the activity context (Lord & Magill, 1989).

In free-play situations, children with autism present varied *social play styles* that are consistent with Wing and Gould's (1979) delineation of social impairments in autism (aloof, passive, active-odd). Children regarded as aloof tend to withdraw or distance themselves from peers while giving the appearance that they are unaware of their presence. Children who tend to be more passive may follow along or watch peers at play, but rarely initiate interaction in an overt way. Children considered active-odd make obvious attempts to engage peers in play, but do so in an awkward or idiosyncratic manner (such as talking excessively about one topic).

Studies have shown that children with autism direct fewer overt social initiations to peers (Sigman & Ruskin, 1999) and inconsistently respond to peers when they initiate with them (Attwood, Frith, & Hermelin, 1988). When they do make attempts to interact with peers, their initiations have a tendency to be subtle, obscure, or poorly timed (Lord & Hopkins, 1986; Lord & Magill, 1989). Problems in verbal and nonverbal communication notably affect capacities to enter, coordinate, and sustain social play with peers (Schuler & Fletcher, 2002; Sigman & Ruskin, 1999).

Despite pervasive problems, there is evidence to suggest that children with autism share many of the same capacities and desires for play, peer-group acceptance, and friendship as those of most other children (Bauminger & Kasari, 2000; Boucher & Wolfberg, 2003; Chamberlain, Kasari, & Rotheram-Fuller, 2007; Jordan, 2003). Nevertheless, there are numerous obstacles that stand in the way of their gaining access to and navigating the play culture. Sacks (1995) interpreted Temple Grandin's experiences in childhood in this way:

> Temple had longed for friends at school . . . but there was something about the way she talked, the way she acted, that seemed to alienate others, so that, while they admired her intelligence, they never accepted her as a part of their community. . . . Something was going on between the other kids, something swift, subtle, constantly changing—an exchange of meanings, a negotiation, a swiftness of understanding so remarkable that sometimes she wondered if they were all telepathic. She is now aware of the existence of these social signals. (p. 272)

One might speculate that the peer group plays a decisive role in exacerbating social isolation in children with autism. How peers interpret and respond to the social, communication, and play behavior of children with autism has an especially profound influence on the extent to which these children will be accepted, rejected, or simply ignored (Heinrichs, 2003; Wolfberg et al., 1999). The failure of peers to appreciate the subtle or idiosyncratic ways in which children with autism convey their interests or intentions widens the gap between them (Wolfberg, McCracken, & Tuchel, 2008).

Personal accounts and studies documenting the experiences of individuals with high-functioning autism and Asperger's reveal hardships and heartbreaks as a result of not having played and formed friendships with peers during childhood (Bauminger & Kasari, 2000; Bemporad, 1979; Chamberlain et al., 2007; Donnelly & Bovee, 2003; Müller, Schuler, & Yates, 2008). Donna Williams (1992) describes the irony of this situation through personal accounts of her own childhood play:

> Other children played school, mothers and fathers, doctors and nurses. Other children skipped ropes and played with balls or swap-cards. I had swap-cards. I gave them away in order to make friends, before learning that I was supposed to swap them, not give them away. (p. 22)

> I often played alone, swinging on the monkey bars, looking at my cards, climbing trees, pulling flowers apart, spinning around and around as I stared up into the sun. I would fall to the ground and watch the world spin. I was in love with life but I was terribly alone. (p. 24)

> I went around the school for weeks asking everyone I came across if they were my friend. . . . Eventually I gave up and sat in a corner of the school ground, against the back fence. After a few months, two girls decided they would let me hang around with them. The things they talked about bored me. I drifted away from them mentally, and soon they, too, drifted away from me. I fell into a deep depression that lasted about a year. I returned to my old school but hung about on the outside of any groups that tried to involve me. I stopped smiling and laughing, and the efforts to involve me only hurt me more, till I'd stand there with tears silently rolling down my face. (p. 39)

SUMMARY

The impulse to play, while not entirely absent, is notably subdued in children with autism as compared with typically developing children. They encounter many struggles in play ranging from communicating an interest in the activities of other children to adopting a nonliteral orientation in pretend. The unusual ways in which they relate to people and objects often excludes them from the culture of play with peers. They may become caught in a cycle of peer exclusion, which deprives them of opportunities to learn to play in more conventional and socially accepted ways. Without the normal childhood experiences of social pretend play, children with autism may become locked in a solitary world of literal meanings. In the following chapter we merge theory with practice, examining ways in which to support the inclusion of children with autism in peer play.

C H A P T E R   5

Play in Practice

> The child shall have full opportunity for play and recreation, which should be directed to the same purpose as education: society and public authorities shall endeavour to promote the employment of this right.
>
> —United Nations, Declaration of the Rights of the Child

PROTECTING THE CHILD'S right to play clearly is not a new concept. Traditionally, this has been a concern of early childhood educators in Western societies (Isenberg & Quisenberry, 2002; Singer et al., 2006). While such organizations as the International Association for the Child's Right to Play are committed to the preservation of play for all children, this has had little impact on the status of play for children with autism.

Conditions suitable for typical children's active engagement in play (such as providing time, space, props, and access to playmates) generally do not suffice for children who lack an apparent predisposition to play. Even with the best of intentions by caring adults, many children with autism continue to be deprived of their basic right to participate fully in the culture of play with peers.

As discussed in previous chapters, having a clear understanding and appreciation of the complex challenges children with autism experience in play is essential for overcoming obstacles to full participation in play. To design truly effective and meaningful play interventions requires bridging the gap between theory and practice. A review of the advancement of play interventions relevant to the design of the Integrated Play Groups model follows.

PLAY INTERVENTIONS

Historically, play has had a relatively limited role in the education and treatment of children with autism. This is rather puzzling, considering that

impoverished play is a hallmark of autism and that there is a vast literature on play's many contributions. In a comprehensive review, Williams
(2003) reported that of 161 studies that make reference to play in autism,
only 7% specifically focus on promoting play. Rather, the majority of these
studies relegate play as a context for targeting other treatment outcomes.

While this general apathy is likely a reflection of prevailing conceptions and social attitudes surrounding the function and value of play, there
are, no doubt, other influential factors emanating from the field of autism.
As we noted in a related work (Wolfberg & Schuler, 2006):

> Particularly when dealing with children whose behaviors defy developmental
> expectations, play is more likely to be viewed as a luxury only to be targeted
> when more basic deficiencies have been remedied. Moreover, the [field's]
> current emphasis on accountability, quantification and empirically validated
> programs may have inadvertently discouraged the pursuit of play in a
> broader developmental and cultural context. (p. 182)

Despite the relative neglect of play, recent advances in autism provide
a glimmer of hope that the field may be shifting in a new direction. As a
major turning point, the National Research Council (2001) ranked the teaching of play skills with peers among the top six areas that should receive
priority in interventions for young children with autism. This conclusion
not only helped to validate past play intervention efforts (including our
own), but also helped to launch new approaches to addressing this area of
need (Boucher & Wolfberg, 2003).

To date, a wide variety of play interventions are among the options
available for children with autism. The approaches taken are highly diverse
in terms of theoretical orientation, goals, methods, and the contexts within
which they are applied. The following provides an overview of the wide
assortment of approaches taken to address play in children with autism.

Traditional and Contemporary Play Therapy

Play therapy is an approach that has been fraught with confusion and controversy as applied to children with autism over the years. While rooted
in the psychoanalytic tradition, there are currently many different forms
of play therapy that greatly vary in perspective (Schaefer & Kaduson, 2007).
Until the 1960s, psychoanalytic approaches prevailed in the treatment of
children classified with a wide range of psychological problems, including children diagnosed with early childhood schizophrenia, or autism, as
we know it today (Axline, 1947; A. Freud, 1946; Klein, 1955). The idea of

traditional play therapy was to draw the child out of his or her "autistic state" by working through internal conflicts that were thought to arise from past experiences, most notably, a dysfunctional mother-child relationship (Mahler, 1952). Purportedly, the child represented and expressed these inner struggles in play. Changing views on autism, which is now more likely to be perceived as an organic- rather than psychogenic-based disorder, clearly underscore the controversy surrounding traditional play therapy (Riddle, 1987).

Although still practiced in some circles, traditional play therapy is no longer a treatment of choice for children with autism. Further, while more contemporary versions of play therapy are widely accepted and practiced with a variety of children, research showing explicit benefits to children with autism is limited (Mittledorf, Hendricks, & Landreth, 2001). Nevertheless, one might presume that there may be potential benefits to children with higher social-cognitive abilities who present emotional difficulties coupled with or as a by-product of autism.

Adult-Directed Approaches

Based on principles of applied behavior analysis (ABA), adult-directed approaches are among the most prevalent play interventions for children with autism (Stahmer, Ingersoll, & Carter, 2003). Discrete trial training (DTT), originally developed by Lovaas (1987), is one of the earliest approaches that continues to be widely practiced today (Leaf & McEachin, 1999; Maurice, Green, & Luce, 1996; Smith, 2001). DTT involves teaching a discrete set of target play behaviors or subskills through a series of repeated training trials. Prompting, reinforcement, and shaping procedures are used to elicit the target response within a highly controlled, adult-driven environment. While studies report variable success (Nuzzolo-Gomez, Leonard, Ortiz, Rivera, & Greer, 2002; Santarcarangelo, Dyer, & Luce, 1987), a major drawback is that the heavy reliance on adult control and high level of structure compromise spontaneous play and generalization to natural environments (Wolfberg & Schuler, 2006).

To address these shortcomings, behavioral approaches have been modified to incorporate more naturalistic and child-centered practices (Lifter, Sulzer-Azaroff, Anderson, & Cowdery, 1993; Stahmer et al., 2003). Notably, Pivotal Response Training (PRT) considers the child's development and motivation by selecting preferred activities while modeling, prompting, and reinforcing reasonable attempts to correctly respond (Koegel, Koegel, Harrower, & Carter, 1999). While PRT has been shown to be successful in promoting manipulation, functional, symbolic, and sociodramatic play, difficulties remain with respect to low levels of spontaneous child initiations and social interaction during play (Stahmer, 1995; Thorp, Stahmer, & Schreibman, 1995).

Child-Centered Approaches

Child-centered approaches, applied within a developmental framework, are gaining popularity among play interventions for children with autism (Boucher & Wolfberg, 2003). Most target young children while facilitated by an adult, one on one. Guided by a careful appraisal of the child's developmental status, a variety of practices are used to promote play behaviors in a sequence that mirrors typical development. To promote early object play, effective practices have included selecting toys and modeling play actions that are carefully matched to the child's interest and developmental level (Hauge, 1988; Van Berckelaer-Onnes, 2003; Williams, 2003). Studies have also reported success using deliberate imitation of the child's spontaneous behavior and actions to elicit joint attention, imitation, and social reciprocity in play (Dawson & Adams, 1984; Ingersoll & Schreibman, 2002; Kalmanson & Pekarsky, 1987; Tiegerman & Primavera, 1981).

These types of practices have been adopted by a wide variety of programs. Floor Time is an approach in which the adult follows the child's lead using gestures, words, and affect to establish joint attention and stimulate increasingly complex social and symbolic play (Greenspan & Wieder, 1997; Wieder & Greenspan, 2003). The Denver model (Rogers et al., 2000) includes a focus on promoting social and toy play through engagement in "sensory social exchanges" centered on the child's toy preferences and social initiations. Sherrat (2002) developed a systematic classroom-based approach that incorporates structure, affect, and repetition to stimulate spontaneous and novel forms of play. The SCERTS (Social Communication, Emotional Regulation and Transactional Support) model offers a framework that includes various dimensions of support while applying similar child-centered practices that serve to promote play (Prizant, Wetherby, Rubin, Rydell, & Laurent, 2003).

Peer-Mediated Approaches

Typically developing peers are increasingly being included as play partners in interventions. Odom and Strain (1984) documented peer-mediated approaches based on behavioral approaches. Accordingly, peers are trained to model, prompt, and reinforce the social and play responses of the child with autism in much the same way as an adult would (Strain et al., 1979; Ragland et al., 1978). While early studies reported increases in the frequency and duration of social interaction (Odom & Strain, 1984), critics point out that improvements did not generalize beyond the peer tutor (Lord & Hopkins, 1986) and that the intervention did not correspond to contexts in which social play naturally occurs (Lord & Magill, 1989).

To remediate problems of generalization and the artificial role of peers, subsequent behavioral interventions have included training both the children with autism and peers (Goldstein & Cisar, 1992; Haring & Lovinger, 1989; Oke & Schreibman, 1990) and carrying out interventions in inclusive settings where peer play naturally occurs (e.g., Pierce & Schreibman, 1997; Roeyers, 1996; Strain & Kohler, 1998). Despite evidence supporting success with these variations, there continues to be a heavy reliance on explicit and precise adult control to effectively deliver the intervention. This type of adult-imposed structure is clearly at odds with inherent qualities of play as intrinsically motivated, governing a self-imposed structure.

Based on systematic comparisons of low versus high levels of adult intrusion on children's spontaneous play with peers (Meyer et al., 1987; Shores, Hester, & Strain, 1976), peer-mediated approaches reflect a trend toward a less adult-imposed structure consistent with child-centered practices. More loosely structured interventions that provide repeated exposure to familiar peers and their play activities with minimal adult involvement have yielded both quantitative and qualitative improvements in the social interaction, language, and play of children with autism (Casner & Marks, 1984; Lord & Hopkins, 1986; McHale, 1983). Moreover, studies comparing structured versus facilitated peer play found that communication and play increased with both techniques; however, the facilitated approach was more effective in eliciting spontaneous communication and play in children with more advanced skills (Bernard-Opitz, Ing, & Kong, 2004; Kok, Kong, & Bernard-Opitz, 2002).

Ecological Considerations

Child-centered approaches closely connect with ecological considerations in the selection of suitable play partners and contexts. Several investigations examined the developmental status of peers as a variable in promoting play and playful interactions. Studies of younger peers, closely matched in developmental age to children with autism, revealed improvements in specific social play behaviors that did not occur with adults of the same chronological age (Bednersh & Peck, 1986; Lord & Hopkins, 1986). Bednersh and Peck (1986) also reported that children with autism displayed more conventional object play while interacting with older typically developing peers and more sensorimotor object play while interacting with younger typically developing peers. These findings suggest that children with autism may benefit in different ways while playing with typically developing peers who are younger, older, and the same chronological age. Children with autism may be more inclined to spontaneously imitate and interact with younger peers who have similar developmental abilities and interests. In contrast, same-age or older peers may be more capable of structuring or scaffolding play events that encourage higher levels of cognitive and social performance.

High degrees of predictability and consistency in the social and physical environment have long been recognized as beneficial for children with autism (Rutter, 1978). Lord and Magill (1989) suggest that providing children with autism opportunities to interact, develop experience, and become familiar with peers contributes to advances in social play. The positive influences of setting variables such as arranging and limiting the size of the physical play space (Phyfe-Perkins, 1980; Smith & Connolly, 1980) and providing specific play materials on the basis of social potential (Beckman & Kohl, 1984), structure (Dewey, Lord, & Magill, 1988), and complexity (Ferrara & Hill, 1980) are also noteworthy considerations.

Many of the interventions reviewed were successful in promoting various aspects of play and social behavior in children with autism, yet none was comprehensive with respect to peer play. The fact that few reported generalized, lasting gains in play does not imply that children with autism are unable to learn how to play. Rather, the interventions narrowly focused on aspects of play, failing to address play in its totality. Focusing on single variables may nevertheless help to determine what variables are necessary for constructing a comprehensive intervention model. To provide sufficient and contextually relevant support to children with autism, all the factors known to affect play must be carefully weighed and considered in the design of such programs.

THE INTEGRATED PLAY GROUPS MODEL

The concept for Integrated Play Groups (IPG) grew in response to the need to develop a comprehensive play intervention for children with autism. The IPG model incorporates variables documented as affecting social interaction, communication, play, and imagination in children on the autism spectrum. The theoretical orientation follows social constructivist and sociocultural conceptions of learning and development extending Vygotsky's perspectives on play as social activity.

"Guided participation" is a major feature of the IPG model. In her cross-cultural research on children's cognitive development, Rogoff (1990) refers to this as the process through which children learn and develop while actively participating in culturally valued activity with the guidance, support, and challenge of partners who vary in skill and status. This process is also similar to Heath's (1989) conception of "the learner as cultural member," Brown and Campione's (1990) "community of learners," and Lave and Wenger's (1991) "legitimate peripheral participation."

In an Integrated Play Group, children with autism (novice players) participate in natural play experiences with typically developing peers (expert players) while supported by an adult (play guide). A major aim is to facilitate mutually enjoyed and reciprocal play among children, while expanding each novice player's social and symbolic play repertoire. Of equal importance is teaching peers to be empathetic, responsive, and accepting of the unique ways in which children with autism relate, communicate, and play. Ultimately, the intent is for children to mediate their own play activities with minimal adult guidance.

Currently, qualified play guides complete a rigorous training program offered by the Autism Institute on Peer Relations and Play. This competency-based program was originally developed, field tested, and evaluated as a part of a model demonstration and training project (Wolfberg & Schuler, 1992) and later updated to coincide with the revision of the IPG field manual (Wolfberg, 2003). The IPG field manual specifically presents principles, tools, and practices for setting the stage for play (program and environmental design), observing children at play (assessment), and guided participation in play (intervention), as summarized below.

Setting the Stage for Play

Planning the program. Professionals and parents collaborate as a team to plan the IPG program. IPGs are customized as a part of a child's individual educational or therapeutic program, which may be carried out in a school, home, or community setting. Each group is composed of three to five children with a higher ratio of expert players (typical peers or siblings) to novice players (children on the autism spectrum). The same group of players meets regularly (2 times per week for 30 minutes to 1 hour) over a 6-month period or longer.

Gathering and preparing the players. Ideally, novice and expert players are familiar and attracted to one another and have the potential to develop long-lasting friendships. Otherwise, expert players may be recruited from existing social networks (school, family friends, neighbors, community centers). Mixing and matching children with respect to gender, ages, developmental status, and social play styles may vary, since there are different benefits in each.

To prepare the players, all the children (novices and experts) participate in "autism demystification" activities that are designed to foster awareness, understanding, and empathy for the unique and diverse ways children with autism may communicate, relate, and play (McCracken, 2005; Wolfberg, McCracken, & Tuchel, 2008).

Preparing the play setting. Several factors are considered in designing the play space and selecting materials. Play areas are purposely contained in size with clear boundaries and explicit organization. Play materials include a wide assortment of highly motivating toys and props that are conducive to stimulating both symbolic and social dimensions of play. The selected materials purposely vary in degree of structure and complexity to accommodate the diverse interests and developmental levels of both the novice and expert players.

Structuring the play session. The structure of the play session is predictable, following a sequence of an opening ritual, guided play, and closing ritual. Visual supports (pictures or written words) are also used to depict the schedule, rules, play choices, play roles, as well as to aid in social communication. The session is also structured for the purpose of establishing group identity and membership. The children come up with names, design posters, create rituals, and engage in other activities that they associate with their particular group.

Observing Children at Play

Becoming a keen observer and interpreter of how children play independently of, beside, and with other children is a fundamental aspect of the play guide role. Assessments provide a basis for setting realistic and meaningful goals, making decisions that guide the intervention, and monitoring children's progress. The IPG model offers tools for recording observations of children's play in a variety of natural play contexts based on the following framework.

Symbolic dimension of play. This refers to play acts that the child directs toward objects, self, or others and that signify events (adapted from McCune-Nicholich, 1981; Piaget, 1962; Smilansky, 1968). The observation domains include no engagement, manipulation play (explores sensory or physical properties of objects), functional play (conventional use of an object or association of two or more objects), symbolic-pretend (represents objects, self, events by substituting, transforming, and inventing, or role playing).

Social dimension of play. This focuses on the child's distance from and involvement with one or more children (adapted from Parten, 1932). These observation domains include isolation (playing alone), orientation-onlooker (watching peers), parallel-proximity (playing beside peers), common focus (reciprocal play with peers in joint activity), common goal (collaborating with peers in an organized fashion.

Communicative functions and means. *Communicative functions* describe what the child intends to convey (for example, requests for objects, peer action, peer assistance, peer interaction, peer affection, protests, declarations, and comments). The functions of communication may be accomplished through a variety of verbal and nonverbal *communicative means* (such as facial expressions; eye gaze; physical proximity; touching; manipulating another's hand, face, or body; showing, giving, or taking objects; enactment of action; gaze shift; gestures; intonation; vocalization; nonfocused or focused echolalia; and simple or complex speech/sign/symbol/written word) (adapted from Peck, Schuler, Tomlinson, Theimer, & Haring, 1984).

Play preferences and diversity of play. Documenting the play preferences of both novice and expert players in play groups offers a means of identifying and matching children's play interests. Play preferences include a child's attraction to toys or props (prefers round objects, toys that move, realistic replicas), interactions with toys or props (prefers to spin toys, to line up toys, to use object conventionally), choice of play activities (prefers roughhousing, quiet play, constructive play), choice of play themes (prefers familiar routines, invented stories, fantasy play), and choice of playmates (prefers no one in particular, one or more specific peers). Documenting the number and variety of play acts offers a means to assess children's diversity of play.

Guided Participation in Play

Guided participation in play is a system of support to help novice and expert players participate in increasingly socially coordinated and sophisticated play activities. The methods used to achieve this system of support are described below.

Monitoring play initiations. Ongoing observations of child initiations in play, even in unusual forms, serve as indices of present and emerging capacities in play. Recognizing and interpreting all play acts as purposeful and adaptive—as meaningful attempts to initiate play with others—or to express oneself in play with materials, roles, and events are essential for guiding decisions on how to intervene on behalf of novice players. Spontaneous, self-generated play initiations represent present interests and capacities in play, while imitative and socially guided play acts represent emerging capacities in play. Play initiations may take many conventional and unconventional forms, including unusual fascinations.

Scaffolding interactions. Scaffolding is the provision of adjustable and temporary support structures. In IPGs, the play guide adjusts the amount of external support provided in relation to the children's play needs. Many children initially require a great deal of assistance while they acclimate to the experience of being in play groups. As the children grow increasingly comfortable and competent in their play, the adult gradually lessens this support and withdraws from the play group. Remaining readily available on the periphery of the group, the adult offers the children a "secure base" from which to explore and try out new activities. At the same time, the adult monitors play initiations and provides assistance whenever necessary.

Social communication guidance. Social communication guidance primarily involves helping the children establish a mutual focus by recognizing and responding to initiations in play. By interpreting the subtle verbal and nonverbal cues of novice players as meaningful and purposeful acts, experts learn to respond and nourish play interactions. By the same token, interpreting by breaking down the complex social cues of expert players allows novices to better understand and fully participate in the play context. Directed to experts and novices alike, social communication guidance fosters attempts to extend invitations to peers to play, persist in enlisting reluctant peers to play, respond to peers' cues and initiations in play, maintain or expand interactions with peers, and join peers in an established play event.

Play guidance. Play guidance focuses on engaging less skilled players in activities slightly beyond their capacity while fully immersed in play. To be fully immersed in play allows children to participate in the whole play experience, even if participation is partial or minimal. Thus novices may carry out play activities and roles that they may not as yet fully comprehend. For example, a child inclined to bang objects may incorporate this scheme into a larger play theme of constructing a building with blocks. With the assistance of more capable peers, the child may take on the role of a construction worker and hammer the blocks with a play tool.

SUMMARY

The interventions reviewed were successful in promoting various aspects of play and social behavior in children with autism. These formed the basis for constructing Integrated Play Groups, a comprehensive play intervention model. This model supports children with autism in mutually enjoyed play experiences with typically developing peers. Novices gain practice and skill while guided by an adult with more capable peers. To guide participation in play the adult monitors, interprets, and builds on children's play interests and social communicative abilities. Even unusual fascinations can be vehicles for socially interactive and imaginative play. The case portraits presented in the following chapters provide a window onto the world of Integrated Play Groups as experienced by Teresa, Freddy, and Jared.

P A R T   I I

Passage to Play Culture:
Ethnographic Case Portraits

CHAPTER 6

Uncharted Territory

TERESA, FREDDY, AND JARED'S case portraits begin with a description of the children and their experiences in early childhood. School records showed that each child had received an independent diagnosis of autism conforming to criteria for autistic disorder within the pervasive developmental disorders spectrum (see Chapter 2). Interviews with family members, former teachers, and therapists confirmed the presence of characteristic features, including onset in the first few years of life; pervasive problems in social interaction, communication, and imaginative activity; and the presence of stereotyped patterns of behavior. Although they had this diagnosis in common, Teresa, Freddy, and Jared naturally had unique identities individually, socially, and culturally.

Teresa is an African American female. She was considered to be an attractive child—tall and lean, a broad face with high cheekbones, and almond-shaped brown eyes that seemed to disappear into slits when she smiled. She proudly wore her wavy brown hair in several ponytails or intricately braided cornrows with beads. She dressed neatly in practical and conservative attire that carried her through each growth spurt.

Teresa grew up in northern California, raised by her mother for the first 5 years of her life and thereafter by her maternal grandmother. She temporarily lived in a foster home while in transition from her mother to her grandmother's custody. She subsequently lived with her grandmother and three uncles in a predominantly African American, working-class, urban neighborhood. Teresa's grandmother, who worked outside the home in an office, owned the modest home in which the family lived. Over the years, Teresa remained in contact with her mother, whom she continues to see on a regular basis. She now has a younger half-brother whom she also regularly visits.

Freddy is a Latino male. He was described as a cute child and reminded me of the character Max in Maurice Sendak's *Where the Wild Things Are*. He was somewhat small in stature, but what he lacked in height he gradually made up for in girth. His round, ruddy face and dark eyes set off his mischievous smile. He wore his thick black hair closely cropped. He dressed comfortably and casually in jeans and sweatshirts, which was typical of his peer group.

An only child, Freddy lived with his mother and father in a culturally diverse, middle-income, urban neighborhood in northern California. His father is a first-generation Mexican American and his mother, a recent immigrant from El Salvador. Freddy was raised in a bilingual household, speaking mainly English with his father and Spanish with his mother. Freddy's father worked as a contractor, while his mother did not work outside the home. The family rented a modest, two-bedroom apartment in a two-story duplex. Growing up, Freddy spent a great deal of time with members of his extended family, including aunts, uncles, and cousins on both sides.

Jared is an African American male. Many people commented on his striking beauty—tall and slender, graceful limbs, a face with soft yet defined features and an often distant expression. His closely shaved hair showed off a perfectly shaped head. Jared, who was nearsighted, wore stylish wire-rimmed glasses in the later half of elementary school. He was always impeccably and fashionably dressed; his shirts and pants, even jeans, were freshly ironed each day.

Jared spent the first 7 years of his life in a rural area of Alabama with his extended family. At the age of 7, he moved with his mother, grandmother, and uncle to northern California, where they lived in a predominantly African American, low-income, urban neighborhood. He was an only child. Although Jared's mother and uncle worked in various positions, the family largely relied on welfare to make ends meet. They rented a small, subsidized apartment that was an extension of a housing project notorious for gang-related crimes. Consequently, Jared rarely was permitted to play outdoors.

ALONE IN THE COMPANY OF CHILDREN

Teresa

Teresa entered a county special education kindergarten for children with autism and related disabilities at the age of 5. At this time she was living in a foster home. She formed attachments with adults, including her teacher and caregivers, but had no known relationships with other children.

Teresa's relationships with adults were somewhat idiosyncratic. She looked to adults for direction and comfort in times of uncertainty, but in a rather circuitous manner. Avoiding face-to-face contact, sustained eye gaze, and displays of physical affection, she often failed to establish a joint reference while communicating her feelings.

Teresa managed to connect with adults on her own terms using alternative means. She often followed and imitated her teacher while performing classroom chores such as cleaning up or preparing meals. She also latched on to adults in unfamiliar situations by holding their hands or grabbing their arms.

During outdoor play at school, Teresa often stayed well inside the playground, maintaining close proximity to her teacher. She rarely displayed interest in her peers and preferred to engage in solitary play activities when encouraged to play. There was a stark quality to her play that accentuated her aloneness.

> Teresa spins slowly in circles alone on a tire swing. Her head is lowered as she gazes downward. A facial expression vaguely resembling a smile remains fixed and unchanging as she spins. Another little boy runs back and forth near Teresa, but she gives no indication that she is aware of his presence. While spinning, Teresa raises her hand to her face and partly covers her eyes as though shutting out the world around her. She continues to shield her eyes with her hand and maintains the same unchanging expression while spinning.

When Teresa went to live with her grandmother at age 6, she entered a special day class for children with autism in an integrated public school, Lewis Elementary. She reconnected with members of her extended family and established new bonds with adults in her classroom. Teresa was especially sensitive to adult reprimands and criticism, particularly when they reacted to her recurrent displays of impulsive acting-out behavior. She frequently screamed and threw tantrums in response to disrupted rituals, changes in the schedule, and specific auditory stimuli. In later years, Teresa expressed great sadness and distress when describing memories of her former teacher placing her in time-out (removing her from the classroom) for her apparent inability to stop carrying out an impulsive act. This procedure apparently had little effect, since Teresa's screams and tantrums generally escalated until she reached a point of utter exhaustion and subsequently repeated the behavior.

Despite their use of what many now consider antiquated and aversive practices, the adults in Teresa's classroom adored her and supported her in other ways. Similarly, Teresa looked up to them and enjoyed being in their company. Her social interest in others, however, was confined exclusively to adults. She showed relatively little interest in her peers for anything other than instrumental purposes. Described as having "motherly type" behavior, Teresa often imitated her teacher by straightening other children's clothes or fixing their hair. When given opportunities for free play, she spent most of her time following and clinging to teachers on the playground or, as in her previous school, pursuing solitary activities.

Freddy

Freddy entered Lewis Elementary School for kindergarten at the age of 5, but enrolled in a different special education class from Teresa's. He too preferred to interact with adults rather than peers. By this time he had established an especially strong attachment to his father, who devoted himself to the role of educating his son. His mother, on the other hand, had difficulty bonding with her son during his early years because of his aloof nature and what she described as his "strong will."

Like Teresa, Freddy displayed signs of impulsive acting-out behavior. He threw many tantrums in response to disruptions in his usual routines and rituals. His insistence on maintaining rituals had an impact on relations with family members. Freddy's parents described feeling stressed as they sought ways to pacify their son.

> Freddy's parents try countless times to get him to eat a different kind of breakfast cereal other than his usual Cheerios. He protests each time they pour a different type of cereal from its box into his bowl. They soon discover that by pouring the new brand of cereal into his Cheerios box, and then pouring this into his bowl, he graciously accepts and eats the cereal. Eventually, Freddy insists that he himself pour the alternate cereal into the Cheerios box and into his bowl before eating. Left with little recourse, Freddy's parents surrender to his idiosyncratic whims.

In school, Freddy and his classroom teacher established a mutual attachment. Describing Freddy as a "warm, affectionate, cooperative, and friendly child," his teacher expressed a great fondness for him. He apparently even favored Freddy over his other students (although not necessarily to their exclusion) and took him out on special outings, including a ski trip. This teacher recounted feelings of great sadness at separating from Freddy when he left his teaching position at the end of the school year.

Although Freddy equally enjoyed his teacher's company, he displayed his affection for him through indirect means. Like Teresa, Freddy expressed an interest in adults by peripherally watching and occasionally imitating their routine activities. He also consistently avoided direct social contact by avoiding face-to-face encounters, averting his eye gaze, and recoiling from physical touch. Unlike Teresa, he rarely sought out adults for comfort in times of stress. His emotional outbursts rarely corresponded to the usual ups and downs or aches and pains of childhood.

Like Teresa, Freddy had limited interaction with his peers as social partners. He expressed apparent interest in his classmates' actions as he peripherally watched them carry out repetitive activities. Yet his only contact with them resulted from his obsession with making sure they adhered to predictable routines without any disruptions. For instance, a classmate's recurrent request to his teacher for a ruler to "measure" the bookcases prompted Freddy to obtain the ruler for his classmate. Other than acting as an intermediary for retrieving and delivering objects, he avoided his peers and remained alone in social play situations.

Jared

Little is known about Jared's social relations with adults and peers prior to the time he moved to California and entered Lewis Elementary School at the age of 7. He had been placed in a "multihandicapped class" at the age of 5 in Alabama, where he initially received special education services. Jared's mother and grandmother recalled that his teacher and classmates were very fond of him. They shared photographs of his school birthday party in which attentive adults and eager children ready to partake of birthday cake surrounded him. Jared's face, however, gave no hint of what he may have been feeling at the time. Considered a very compliant child who occasionally had "attitude problems," he passively went along with whatever adults intended for him to do as long as he understood their directions. More often than not, however, Jared failed to understand complex directions and was said to "get lost in the shuffle."

While his mother and grandmother lavished a great deal of endearments upon him, Jared gave little back in terms of any signs of physical affection or even simple pleasure. Unlike Freddy and Teresa, Jared willingly engaged in face-to-face contact and sustained eye gaze with familiar adults. However, his total passivity and lack of affect made it very difficult for others to interpret his wants, needs, and emotional responses.

Jared's only clear emotional signals were his protests to certain events. Like Freddy, he often recoiled from physical touch and resisted attempts to hold his hand. Like Teresa, he was particularly sensitive to certain sounds and emitted screams or held his ears to block out the sensation. He frequently displayed outbursts of screaming, hand flapping, and hitting himself on the head when subjected to certain types of visual and auditory stimuli. To control this behavior, his caregivers gave him simple commands to stop jumping or keep his hands down. Despite Jared's lack of overt social responding, he clearly reacted idiosyncratically to familiar adults as he looked to them for cues to regulate his own behavior.

One might speculate that Jared, like Teresa and Freddy, expressed little social interest in other children. He apparently spent time with cousins of younger and similar ages but never developed any particular alliances. When he began school in California, he responded indifferently to other children and their activities. The rather sparse and deficient quality of Jared's Individualized Educational Plan (IEP) from his previous school led to a similar deduction concerning his dearth of peer relationships. The objectives outlined in this document focused exclusively on independent tasks, with no mention of social skills of any kind, not even in conjunction with his speech, language, and communication goals. The omission of social skills objectives may have reflected a lack of understanding of the nature of Jared's disability rather than his proficiency in this domain.

CREATING ORDER THROUGH RITUALS

Teresa

Teresa had a limited repertoire of spontaneous play activities, characterized as repetitive and unimaginative. She carried out stereotyped play acts for extended periods of time. She routinely manipulated objects on the basis of common features, such as lining up or stacking all red blocks. She also performed rituals around acquired fascinations, such as ceaselessly combing a doll's hair.

Teresa apparently understood the function of objects and the conventions of familiar routines but was as yet unable to pretend. While she systematically applied common schemes beyond herself to dolls, such as the familiar act of combing hair, she failed to recognize the doll as a social object. Her interactions with dolls were stark in comparison to those of typical children. She never held the doll as though it were a baby, gazed at the doll with a look of endearment, or talked or otherwise vocalized to it in any way to indicate pretending. In essence, the doll was no different from the other children in Teresa's class whose clothing she helped to readjust.

At the age of 7, Teresa developed a play ritual emerging from a fascination with underclothing and jewelry. She often approached adults to touch their jewelry and explore beneath their outerwear. She also spent extended periods of time fixating on pictures that displayed items that fascinated her.

Teresa sits alone in a partitioned area of the classroom. She flips through a Sears clothing catalog, glancing at a few specific pages. These pages are filled with photographs of women's underclothing symmetrically displayed in rows and columns. While gazing at the pictures, she repeatedly utters the word "bra-a-a" in a long, drawn-out, and high-pitched voice. After each utterance she giggles excitedly.

Freddy

Freddy's repertoire of spontaneous play activity was also repetitive and unimaginative in nature. His play routines revolved around behavior involving self-stimulation and the manipulation of objects. Notably, Freddy engaged in the repeated and lengthy ritual of banging his chin with his fist and various objects. This act apparently accelerated during times of social isolation and stress, resulting in a rather conspicuous callous beneath his chin. Concern that Freddy might seriously injure himself led to instituting an annual IEP goal to extinguish this behavior in his first year of school: "Freddy will refrain from banging objects against his chin for periods of up to 1 hour." While his teacher, speech and language therapist, and other classroom staff were responsible for implementing this goal, there was no mention of the procedures they used. Whatever methods they did employ were apparently unsuccessful, since the identical goal was repeated in the subsequent year and Freddy continued to exhibit this behavior until the time that I became his teacher.

Freddy engaged in other types of perseverative play activity, including bouncing a ball close against himself and various flat surfaces. He especially enjoyed playing ball in his backyard while watching his neighbor's dog from a distance. He was also fascinated with water and liked to open the lid of the washing machine while it was in operation. He derived great pleasure from long periods of water play in the sink or bathtub, gazing as wet streams flowed from the faucet through his fingers and down the drain. He enacted a similar ritual in which he sifted sand and other small objects through his fingers, observing the piles form below.

Jared

Jared's spontaneous play likewise lacked diversity and imagination. It is unclear whether he understood the conventional uses of most objects, since he rarely initiated interactions with toys and other materials. His interests were uniquely limited to visually stimulating events involving flashes of movement, color, and letters of the alphabet, and to listening to music consisting of simple songs and rhythms. Needless to say, watching *Sesame Street* on television was one of his favorite pastimes. He displayed a number of rituals associated with his excitement and stimulation, including clapping his hands, flapping his arms, screaming, and jumping in the air. He also took great pleasure in chasing birds so that he could watch them take off and fly in the air. He often attempted to touch them and give them a swift push with his hand as if to make them go faster. The movement of motor vehicles and of people bicycling, roller-skating, or briskly walking all held similar fascination for Jared.

IMITATING SOUNDS AND SIGNS

Teresa

Teresa had virtually no language until the age of 5, although she was known to loudly scream, squeal, and repeatedly utter certain sounds (such as *beep, beep, beep*). Around the age of 6, she began to echo sounds and eventually words, producing them in a loud and high-pitched tone. By age 7, she had incorporated immediate and delayed echolalic utterances into her repertoire. She often repeated single words—mainly nouns—and unintelligible vocalizations in combination with actions. She also combined portions of other people's statements into new and relevant remarks, known as mitigated echolalia. About 75% of Teresa's utterances were considered contextually appropriate and conversational in style.

   During this same period, Teresa's teacher described her as at a "readiness" level in reading and writing. Teresa tested at a kindergarten level in a formal inventory of basic development in reading/reading readiness and comprehension. She could identify and copy letters of the alphabet as well as her name.

Freddy

Freddy was also nonverbal prior to entering kindergarten. He began to spontaneously echo single words in a whisper during his first year in school. By approximately age 7, he would consistently whisper one- and two-word utterances to name familiar objects and make requests when prompted. According to speech therapist reports, despite his poor articulation and vocal delivery, his speech was 80% intelligible within known contexts. In addition, he was learning that speech could result in pleasant consequences. IEP goals thus focused on "expanding Freddy's verbal repertoire, urging Freddy to voice requests for desired objects and activities, and encouraging meaningful verbal attempts through praise." Freddy undoubtedly achieved this in prompted situations as the length and complexity of his utterances gradually increased. His spontaneous speech, however, remained whispered and limited to one- and two-word echolalic utterances. In direct conflict with earlier interventions, Freddy's IEP in the following year stressed "suppressing" rather than encouraging his echolalia. In other words, his spontaneous echoes were not seen as meaningful attempts to communicate.

Freddy's father claimed to have spent a great deal of time reading to him before the boy entered kindergarten. While in school, Freddy exhibited the ability to recognize and memorize numerous written words from product labels advertised in brochures and from various shows listed in the television guide. By age 7, he had a sight reading vocabulary of about 100 words, recognized his written name, identified and recited letters of the alphabet, and traced letters of the alphabet using models. In the following year, his sight vocabulary reportedly increased to more than 150 words and included simple sentences describing action pictures.

Jared

Little is known about Jared's early patterns of speech development except that he, like Teresa and Freddy, had little language at the time he entered kindergarten. He, too, began to echo single-word responses, but he had a great deal more difficulty articulating sounds than did Teresa and Freddy. By approximately age 7, his vocalizations consisted of tongue clicking, exaggerated lallations (substituting the phoneme /l/ for /r/), and high-pitched noises. His attempts to imitate single words were considered intelligible less than 10% of the time.

Jared developed an early fascination with letters of the alphabet and simple written words by having books read to him and watching his favorite television show, *Sesame Street*. Like Teresa, he tested around kindergarten level in reading/reading readiness when he was approximately 7 years. His comprehension, however, was significantly lower than preschool level. He apparently memorized a number of words from books, recognized his written name, and identified and recited letters of the alphabet.

INTERPRETIVE SUMMARY

In their early childhood years, Teresa, Freddy, and Jared were generally apathetic toward peers; instead they focused on objects and familiar adults in their social environment. Adults played instrumental roles in providing these children's wants and needs, including creating a certain degree of order, predictability, and security. Unable to sort out the complexities of social behavior and sensory stimuli, each child sought to control the forces of the physical world. They created order through carrying out repetitive activities based on peculiar fascinations with creatures and things. At the same time, the roots of language and symbolic understanding tentatively began to appear as they imitated sounds and reproduced graphic images encountered in their daily lives.

C H A P T E R   7

Beginning to Explore

TERESA, FREDDY, AND JARED were 7 years of age when I began as a special education teacher in the "autistic program" at Lewis Elementary School. This school was situated in a quiet, sprawling, middle-income neighborhood whose residents were predominantly Asian. The school served approximately 350 students from kindergarten through fifth grade. The school's population was relatively diverse, with many students bused from different parts of the city through the district's policy of creating racially and ethnically balanced schools.

My class consisted of nine students with autism and related special needs ranging in age from 7 to 11 years. The children had a range of abilities and varied ethnic, cultural, and socioeconomic backgrounds, reflecting the school's general population and the communities in which they lived.

My class was well staffed. I was fortunate in having three instructional assistants, one assigned full time to a boy with intensive needs. I worked closely with a speech therapist, occupational therapist, and adaptive physical education instructor. As crucial members of the IEP team, the families played a major role in obtaining these and other services for their children.

Our first year together at Lewis Elementary School was my initiation into the public school system. I was pleased to participate in the school's integration and "mainstreaming" (now referred to as "inclusion") efforts, though I had little knowledge and experience in that regard. There were two other established special education classes on the school's campus that I initially looked to as models. Mirroring the schedules of these two other classes, the children in my class spent the majority of the school day in our special education classroom, joining their peers from the general education classes mainly for lunch, recess, and physical education.

Placing a high value on play, literacy, and creative expression, I consciously immersed the children in these types of activities throughout the school day. Enhancing communication and socialization was central to everything we did together. I attempted to create a highly visual, predictable, and organized environment by assigning picture-word cues to physical space, materials, schedules, activities, and events. Within this framework, the children had multiple opportunities to read, write, draw, paint, and play independently and with peers. The guidance I provided was largely experimental, drawing on personal experience, intuition, and a growing knowledge of theory and practice. Like Teresa, Freddy, and Jared, I was beginning to explore their social and symbolic worlds.

NOTICING OTHER CHILDREN

Teresa

Teresa had difficulty making the transition to my classroom at the start of the school year. She frequently cried for her former teacher and repeated the names of her past classmates. She soon grew accustomed to the new classroom environment, however, bonding with me and other staff members.

Perhaps as an expression of her fondness for us, Teresa perpetually mimicked the adults in our class. As she had done with former teachers, she imitated acts associated with classroom chores and caring for the other children. She often parroted adult conversations, miming gestures, facial expressions, laughter, and certain qualities of speech. While amused and even embarrassed by these impersonations and parodies, I construed these performances as serious attempts to make sense of her environment. Imitation was a powerful medium through which Teresa began to explore the physical and social world.

Teresa's earlier fascinations with jewelry and underclothing persisted and grew into a more pronounced obsession. She developed a particular fascination with large stomachs and breasts, occasionally touching children and women to expose these body parts. Although my staff and I did not encourage this, for obvious reasons, we viewed this behavior as a manifestation of Teresa's curiosity about people, an important attainment that could be redirected and nurtured through more socially acceptable means.

Early in the school year, Teresa actively avoided peer interaction on the playground and in other free play situations. She persistently clung to familiar adults, sometimes hiding behind them when children approached her. As an indication of extreme shyness, she frequently shielded her eyes with her hand in the presence of other children. Initially, she resisted efforts to bring her into activities with other children by screaming, crying, and latching on to adults for protection and comfort.

We attempted to orient Teresa to the other children as she clung to us at recess. We encouraged her to watch peers at play, pointing out individual children by name and describing their activities. Once Teresa ceased to recoil behind her adult escorts, we modeled brief social exchanges with other children by waving hello and engaging them in conversations about their activities. Teresa eventually let go of our hands and began to wander and watch the other children on her own. Still remaining somewhat aloof, she began to wave and say hello to certain children from a distance. With adult assistance, she learned to participate in play activities with other children for brief periods of time.

Freddy

Freddy also grew very attached to the adults in our classroom at Lewis Elementary School. Initially, he acted somewhat shy and even fearful in social situations. In addition to averting his eyes and resisting physical touch, Freddy avoided social contact by purposefully falling off his chair and hiding beneath furniture. Rather than battle with him each time this occurred, we gave Freddy the space he needed, trying to motivate him to join his peers in class. By our playfully teasing, tickling, and instigating social games of peekaboo and hide-and-seek, he began to respond to our social bids.

Freddy soon welcomed physical contact with adults in the classroom. His desire and need to be hugged and held arose during periods of high stress in which he reacted fitfully to intrusions on routines and rituals. On one such occasion, our class was on an outing in the community.

> I prepare Freddy and several other classmates for a journey into the community using a picture-word schedule denoting the bus we would take back to school. Due to unforeseen circumstances, we are forced to take an alternate bus route, which means walking several blocks to another bus stop. Upon realizing this stroke of fate, Freddy begins to panic. His face rapidly changes to a deep shade of red, and his eyes swell with tears. Freddy lets out a hushed cry and throws himself to the ground. Seeing this, I quickly lift him off the ground and hold him in my arms like a baby. I feel Freddy instantly relax in my hold, his rapid pulse gradually growing calmer as I carry him down the street. Once we reach the next bus stop, Freddy breaks free of my hold, racing to be first in line to enter the bus.

Freddy's anxiety in dealing with changes in his environment led to many such instances of gaining my full attention. My reaction was intuitive, far removed from the tenets dominating theory and practice in special education ("Thou shalt not reinforce inappropriate behavior"). I interpreted Freddy's panic-stricken behavior as a call to comfort him, to offer solace not unlike the comfort one might give to a small child in a frightening situation.

From such experiences, Freddy soon learned that his behavior could have an effect on others and that he could even manipulate the situation to his advantage. He began to throw tantrums in a predictable fashion, scripting them into his daily routine. Clearly, his cries no longer carried the same message. It wasn't long before Freddy realized that he could gain attention from others by voicing his wants, desires, and protests through more conventional and playful means.

Like Teresa, Freddy strengthened his connection to the adults around him through imitation. He mimicked their language, gestures, facial expressions, and a variety of social routines involving affectionate displays and playful interactions. One such routine stemmed from his recurrent pattern of intensely watching me while I appeared not to be looking.

> Through my peripheral vision I detect Freddy intensely watching me. When I think I can catch his eyes, I quickly turn and look at Freddy looking at me. I say teasingly, "I caught you looking at me." At this moment, Freddy averts his gaze but continues to watch me out of the corner of his eyes, laughing. I join him in laughter, repeating the sequence over again.

To achieve a similar response, Freddy began calling out my name, averting his eyes, and laughing at the critical moment. He later extended this game by echoing television commercials. He also derived great pleasure from sneaking up behind me and tickling me on the nape of my neck or under my arm. Once he gently pushed me off my chair, sat down in my place, and patted his lap to gesture where I should sit. Toward the end of the school year, he initiated hugs with me and other familiar adults by pointing to himself and saying, "Me, baby me."

Initially, Freddy remained aloof in the company of his peers. He typically chose solitary activities during free play in the classroom and on the playground. When left to his own devices, he carried a ball while wandering aimlessly around the playground, swinging on the swings, and riding a tricycle. As with Teresa, we attempted to engage Freddy in activities with peers. He largely ignored our efforts but nevertheless began to take notice of the other children and their games. He developed an especially keen interest in his classmate Jared, who began chasing Freddy while he rode his tricycle on the playground.

Eventually, Freddy began to spontaneously initiate chase and tag games with other children. To keep the interaction going, however, he required the assistance of an adult to guide each step along the way. At the end of the school year, children from a second-grade class invited to Freddy to join them in an ongoing game of sock ball. While Freddy looked forward to this as a routine event, he had difficulty participating in the actual game. Instead, he persistently ran away from his peers in the hopes that they would chase him.

Jared

Of the three children, Jared was perhaps the most enigmatic in terms of his social behavior. When he first entered my class, he reacted with great apprehension when we approached him. He frequently screamed when an adult or classmate touched him or took him by surprise. On one occasion he even slapped a staff person when she moved toward him in an abrupt manner. For the most part, however, he was extremely passive and compliant, showing little affect or expression on his face.

Once Jared grew accustomed to the classroom routine, he began to interact with adults for instrumental purposes. He soon figured out that through adults he could anticipate fairly predictable responses as well as access a variety of enjoyable activities. During circle time he engaged me in finger-play songs by physically manipulating my mouth and hands. When finishing an assignment, he held up his product to receive his usual "Good job" and happy-face insignia. Like both Teresa and Freddy, Jared began to actively imitate me in these routine situations by mimicking my language, gestures, facial expressions, and actions in anticipation of the predicted outcome. He thus began praising himself and drawing happy faces on all his own work. At a certain point he seemed almost fused with me to the extent that he actually initiated shaking his own hand and confused his name with mine.

Jared gradually accepted and displayed physical affection with adults in the class. He often requested hugs and permission to sit on my lap, particularly during story time. He occasionally solicited hugs by saying, "Baby," perhaps having learned this from his classmate Freddy. His affect improved slightly, with occasional bursts of spontaneous smiles and laughter during social exchanges. When overwhelmed in a crowded place or upset by an unusual event, Jared sought me out for a comforting hug. He whimpered like a baby when he hurt himself, displaying the wounded area for the usual kiss and "All better now."

Emanating from his fascination with visually stimulating events and maintaining certain routines, Jared began to take notice of his peers in a rather peculiar fashion. He was keen to make sure that children walking in lines kept moving right along. He attempted to give children a little push to maintain their rhythm and flow down the hallways. Similarly, he often prompted peers to stick to certain routines by physically manipulating their materials (turning on a record player, putting toothpaste on a toothbrush).

On the playground, birds held more of a fascination for Jared than did his peers—until he discovered Freddy. Jared's fascination with movement made Freddy and his tricycle a likely candidate for interaction.

> Freddy rides the tricycle with his red ball under one arm. Spotting him from a distance, Jared runs to catch up with him. He stands on the rear platform of the tricycle while Freddy navigates the playground. Jared jumps off the platform, pushes Freddy, screams, and claps while watching him rush into the distance. Freddy turns to look back at Jared. Jared runs to catch up with him and start the ritual over.

Jared instigated this scream-and-chase routine for weeks on end, never tiring. After some time, he spontaneously followed and initiated interactions with Freddy in other social situations. Freddy reciprocated only occasionally, when they discovered a common interest in familiar scenarios. For instance, Jared urged Freddy to read the labels and charts situated around the classroom by physically placing his finger on each word. This was a common event generally prompted by teachers. These types of exchanges, however, were mostly short-lived. Only with extensive adult support could Jared participate in longer social exchanges with other children, such as taking turns in simple songs and games.

RITUALIZING FAMILIAR ROUTINES

Teresa

Teresa's play repertoire initially remained unchanged from the previous year. She continued to organize objects by common features and to repeat the ritual of combing a doll's hair. With our guidance, however, she began to extend her play repertoire, incorporating new schemes and a larger array of toys and activities. By midyear, her play began to change in several ways.

For the first time, Teresa became attached to a particular doll. She insisted on carrying her doll everywhere and keeping it in her cubby at the end of the school day. She began to extend familiar routines to play activities with the doll. To assist her in elaborating play themes, I provided additional props and modeled novel actions. Eventually, Teresa extended the ritual of combing the doll's hair by incorporating a sequence of related bathing and grooming schemes.

> Teresa carries her unclothed doll to the classroom sink, repeating the phrase "Take a bath." With the doll under her arm, she fills a bucket with water and dish soap, calling it "bubble bath." She submerges the doll in water, lifts it out, takes a bottle of shampoo, and squeezes shampoo onto its hair. She scrubs the doll's hair, repeating the phrase "Wash a hair." Teresa dunks the doll in the bucket, lifts it out, and rinses the doll's hair with fresh water. She next takes a towel and wraps it around the doll with the head exposed. From a cupboard, she takes out a hair dryer, plugs it into a socket, and dries the doll's hair, repeating the phrase "Dry a hair." She next takes her doll to the play corner and sits on the floor, placing the doll on her lap. She takes out the comb while holding a portion of the doll's hair in one hand and repeats the phrase "Brush a hair." She combs and braids the doll's hair in sections.

Teresa's doll play still remained starkly unimaginative. While replicating a familiar exchange between caregiver and child, she neglected to engage the doll in social interplay. She never talked to the doll as a caregiver would to a child. Nor did she animate the doll with sounds or movements as one would expect of a baby or child. She continued to regard the doll merely as an object on which she could perform a sequence of familiar actions.

Freddy

Freddy's play interests corresponded to his earlier preoccupation with particular objects and activities. He still fixated on spherical objects, such as balls, balloons, and plastic fruits. He manipulated these objects by incorporating them into some rather complex self-stimulatory sequences. He often flicked and tapped them with his fingers and banged them on his chin. He also maintained an avid interest in media advertisements, therefore remaining fixated on commercial products. He continued to engage in ritualistic play with water and sifting sand and small objects through his fingers.

> Freddy sits cross-legged in a sandbox surrounded by various toys . . . a shovel, bucket, flour sifter, and miniature vehicles. Ignoring

these toys, he scoops up a pile of coarse sand with both hands clasped together. He gazes into his hands; his eyes and mouth gradually open wider and wider as the bits of sand slowly flow through his fingers. He brings his hands closer to his face, staring at the granules with a glazed look in his eyes. He then separates his hands and releases the last bits of sand from his grasp. He closes his mouth while slowly flicking his fingers above the newly formed sand heap.

Freddy occasionally spontaneously inspected and manipulated other toys and props, including cars and small dolls, but his attention generally lapsed after a short while. When supported by an adult, however, Freddy could sustain his attention for longer periods. In addition, he displayed the capacity to use objects in functional play, such as putting a telephone to his ear or play food to his mouth. With initial guidance, he even joined Teresa in giving the baby doll a bath. His fascination with water extended to taking water into his mouth and spitting it onto the doll to rinse off the soapy bubbles. He later imitated the entire bathing sequence from shampooing to blow drying the doll's hair. Needless to say, Freddy repeated this play sequence so often that the baby doll's hair fried into a spiky tangle. As he did his little red ball, Freddy carried this doll under his arm from time to time, but only when Teresa's attention wasn't on the doll.

Jared

Jared still had very little motivation to play with constructive or dramatic toys of any kind. When given the opportunity, he consistently gravitated toward several favorite activities that corresponded to his preoccupation with movement, music, reading, writing, and painting. He often required prompts to gather and arrange materials as well as to get started on a preferred play activity. Once his things were all in place, he would carry out some rather elaborate and perseverative routines. Writing on the chalkboard was one such pleasure he frequently pursued.

Jared passively stands by the chalkboard, glancing momentarily at me. He licks his finger and runs it over the dusty surface, creating a wet, dark streak. He again looks at me and strains to articulate the word "chalkboard." I point to the chalk on the tray below the chalkboard and tell Jared that he may use it to write or draw. Jared immediately picks up the chalk and begins to write sequences of

Plate 1.
Self-Portrait
in Tempera
(Teresa, Age 9)

Plate 2.
Camera
in Crayon
(Teresa, Age 9)

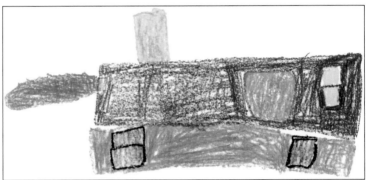

Plate 3.
First Rainbow
Design in Tempera
(Freddy, Age 8)

Plate 4.
Variation of
a Rainbow
in Tempera
(Freddy, Age 8)

Plate 5.
Self-Portrait
as Grownup
in Color Pencil
(Teresa, Age 9)

Plate 6.
Home and
Family
Members
in Crayon
(Teresa, Age 10)

Plate 7.
Illustrations from
"Dora the Star Fish"
in Color Pencil
(Teresa, Age 10)

Plate 8.
Flowers in
Water-Base Marker
(Freddy, Age 9)

Plate 9.
Emily,
Video Camera
and Tripod
in Crayon
(Freddy, Age 9)

Plate 10.
Self-Portrait with
Family Members
in Crayon
(Freddy, Age 9)

Plate 11.
Self-Portrait on a Picnic
in Water-Base Marker
(Freddy, Age 10)

Plate 12.
Self-Portrait Ice Skating
in Pencil and Crayon
(Freddy, Age 10)

numbers . . . 5s, 10s, 100s, and 1,000s. His pace quickens as he rapidly covers the entire surface, moving his body in a kind of rhythmic dance. Upon finishing, he points to each number and reads it aloud.

When Jared's favorite activities were not readily available, he seemed at a loss what to do. In such cases, he typically sat alone staring at nothing in particular until some stimulating event or sensation caught his attention. To engage in any sort of object play, Jared needed coaching. In such cases, he reacted only to concrete materials that could be predictably fashioned into a shape or pattern. He submitted to such tasks as putting together simple puzzles or placing pegs into a board. I occasionally coaxed him to squeeze Play-Doh between his hands or roll a car over the table, but this he did rather unenthusiastically. Only once did Jared spontaneously pick up a baby doll and inspect it.

DISCOVERING MEANING IN WORDS AND PICTURES

Teresa

Teresa's repertoire of echolalic speech increased over the course of the school year. She initially repeated strings of words and phrases in an extremely loud and high-pitched voice. In one instance, she developed a ritualized response to her tremendous fear of the seagulls encountered daily on the school playground. Screaming, she repeated the phrase "Birds a bite" over and over. Rather than endeavor to eliminate this response (a common practice in many special education programs at the time), I sought to extend her linguistic repertoire through social conversation. I responded to Teresa's echoed phrases in the following way.

> TERESA: (*Frightened.*) Birds a bite.
> PAMELA: (*Reassuring.*) Birds won't bite you.
> TERESA: (*Questioning.*) Birds won't bite you?
> PAMELA: (*Affirming.*) That's right; birds won't bite you.
> TERESA: (*With resolution.*) Birds won't bite you.

Although Teresa never overcame her fear of birds, she gained a sense of control over external events through language. To reassure herself, she repeated the phrases she had learned in social conversation. Once, as a joke, I told Teresa, "Birds won't bite you because they don't have teeth." From then on, Teresa adopted this as the phrase she routinely used in her confrontations with seagulls. (Some time later, she discovered the humor in this as well). In a similar manner, Teresa began to use immediate and delayed forms of self-directed echolalia as a mechanism to guide her actions. For instance, she'd repeat the direction "Time to clean up" while cleaning up her area.

Teresa learned to read and write at an exceedingly fast pace. She devised strategies that enabled her to discover meaning in the written word. She began to read and write by copying familiar signs in the classroom. Eventually, she reproduced these signs from memory (see Figure 7.1). Teresa also simulated cursive handwriting (see Figures 7.2 and 7.3). By the end of the school year, she independently wrote in her journal. Each entry typically pertained to a familiar routine or personal life event. She consistently spoke aloud as she wrote, repeating each word or phrase several times. She often inserted echolalic phrases unrelated to the event (see Figure 7.4).

Teresa's development in drawing and painting paralleled her development in language, reading, and writing. She experimented with form and color in her early paintings, repeating a cube-design theme with little variation. Her drawings and paintings progressed over the course of the year from primitive to more naturalistic representations of human figures and familiar objects. Figure 7.4 and Plate 1 show simple transformations in her execution of self-portraits. Plate 2 and Figure 7.5 show realistic renderings of a camera and school bus. While overall her drawings and paintings showed an increasing sense of organization and cohesion of various

Figure 7.1. Sign Reproduced from Memory (Teresa, Age 8)

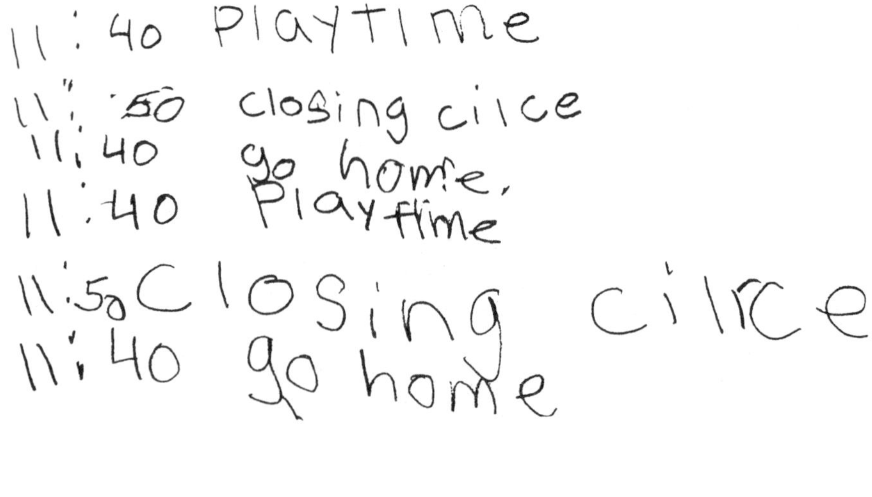

Figure 7.2. Simulated Handwriting (Teresa, Age 8)

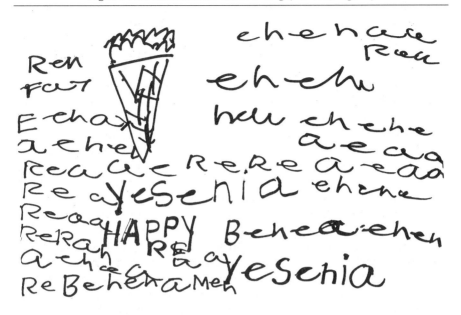

elements, they lacked a sense of personal expression and imagination. She appeared to capture an image as though it were a visual snapshot of the physical world.

Freddy

Freddy increased his production of more communicative forms of echolalic speech over the course of the school year. Rather than "suppress" his echolalia as earlier suggested, I sought to capitalize on Freddy's spontaneous utterances by interpreting them as meaningful expressions. By my doing so, he began to expand his linguistic repertoire, using words and phrases to make requests and to protest.

Freddy also increased his volume from a faint whisper to a more audible tone. The first time he ever spoke above a whisper occurred during what must have been a rather frightening ordeal for him.

During free play, one of Freddy's classmates, a 10-year-old boy of rather large stature, chases him into the closet and accidentally locks him inside. Presuming Freddy had ventured onto the playground, I send out my troops to search for him. After several

Figure 7.3. Independent Journal Entry (Teresa, Age 9)

Figure 7.4. Self-Portrait in Pencil (Teresa, Age 8)

Figure 7.5. School Bus in Water-Base Marker (Teresa, Age 9)

minutes in this predicament, I hear a faint, high-pitched squeak of a voice calling to me from the closet, "Pa-el-am . . . Pa-el-am." Freddy had actually inverted the letter-sounds of my name, Pamela, coming up with this configuration. From that moment on, everyone knows that Freddy can most certainly talk above a whisper.

After this incident, Freddy made an incredible leap in using his voice to communicate a number of stored words and phrases. He was beginning to understand the impact of his language on bringing about change in his environment. He combined single words into novel phrases to express his desire to go somewhere or participate in an event, such as "I go class," "I go outside," and "I want take to office." He also frequently echoed phrases from television commercials and game shows. Although more complex than single words, these types of utterances were contextually dependent and associated with familiar routines.

As Freddy's spoken language increased, his reading and writing also improved. By the end of the school year, he was reading between a first- and second-grade level. His sight vocabulary more than doubled from the previous year, averaging 315 out of 400 tested words. Formal assessments likely underestimated the true number of words Freddy recognized, since he greatly enjoyed reading advertisements, labels on commercial products, the television guide, and the telephone book in his free time.

Freddy learned how to write during this school year. His early writing resembled his first words, particularly in the way he initially inverted the letters of my name. For instance, he had difficulty placing the letters of his own name in the right sequence. Once he managed to put the letters of his entire name in the correct order, he struggled with organizing the space and fitting it onto a page. Freddy gradually learned how to write many of the words and phrases that had become a part of his working vocabulary. With assistance, he was later able to write sentences dictated to him.

Freddy's first paintings consisted of a series of rainbow themes in which he experimented with different colors, allowing them to bleed together (see Plates 3 and 4). His first portraits resembled the happy faces I drew for him on his papers when we worked together (see Figure 7.6). By the end of the school year, he was able to depict human figures performing actions with some coaching, including a portrait of what he wanted to be when he grew up, along with a dictated written description (see Figure 7.7).

Figure 7.6. Happy Face Portrait in Pencil (Freddy, Age 8)

Figure 7.7. Man Painting a Wall, in Crayon (Freddy, Age 9)

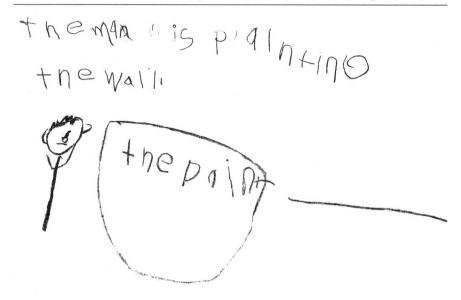

Jared

Jared developed the ability to communicate more effectively during the school year. He began by spontaneously echoing single words combined with simple gestures to indicate his wants and needs. He later learned to combine two words using the "verb (+) noun" structure (for example, "Want music," "Open juice") and to protest by saying, "No." In speech therapy, he learned to label more than 75 object pictures and describe 25 action pictures but was unable to generalize this knowledge to everyday language use. His expressive use of vocabulary remained dependent on contexts and cues, and his receptive language was well below a 3-year-old age level. Even to follow simple one-step commands (for instance, "Sit down") he relied on visual cues such as a speaker's eye gaze.

Jared's articulation showed evidence of severe oral apraxia, with irregular consonant substitutions and distortions, as well as substitution of /a/ for most vowels. Through the use of visual models involving pictures and the printed word, his productions improved. However, he rarely used visual models spontaneously to help himself in sounding out the word or pointed to the word or picture to make a request. To repair failed communicative attempts, Jared consistently used nonverbal means, including putting his face close to mine, rolling his eyes, vocalizing humming sounds, and touching my face while pulling on my hands.

Creating a contrast with his limited understanding and use of spoken language, he excelled in reading and writing. He advanced in reading recognition by about 2 years; however, his comprehension lagged far behind. Some educators might describe Jared as having "hyperlexia." His precocious decoding ability most likely derived from his fascination with the written word in the world around him. His favorite television program was the game show *Jeopardy*, which thrilled him with its flashing words and phrases. Whenever the opportunity arose, he voraciously read and reread every book ever shared with him. He rarely initiated reading unfamiliar books independently. On visits to the library, where he was expected to pick out new books, he implored me to read them to him several times before attempting to read them on his own.

Jared's early paintings included a series of lines in black and a series in color that resembled Teresa's and Freddy's early style (see Figure 7.8). When given free rein to write and draw, Jared typically scribbled known

Figure 7.8. Line Design in Black Tempera (Jared, Age 8)

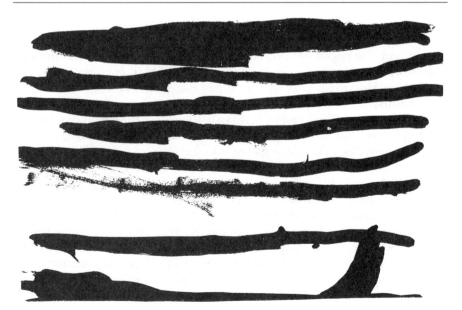

Figure 7.9. "Zippy" Repetitive Graphic Display
in Water-Base Marker (Jared, Age 8)

words and uncomplicated drawings in a repetitive fashion, covering an entire page (see Figures 7.9 and 7.10). Like Freddy, he was fond of mimicking the happy faces I placed as a stamp of approval on his finished work. His portraits of himself and others consisted of just that, simple happy faces lacking in any detail (see Figure 7.11). By the end of the school year, Jared wrote simple dictated sentences and produced more detailed portraits with coaching from me.

INTERPRETIVE SUMMARY

Teresa, Freddy, and Jared began to explore while engaged in playful activity. They initially imitated familiar adults. With adult guidance, they gradually began to take notice of other children. Their attraction to peers and their play activities corresponded to their uniquely formed fascinations with and curiosities about the way people and things functioned. With adult support, they occasionally interacted with peers. They also showed

Figure 7.10. Happy Face Scribble Drawing
in Water-Base Marker (Jared, Age 8)

Figure 7.11. Self-Portrait in Crayon (Jared, Age 9)

a certain degree of exploratory behavior in their independent play activities. Continuing to revolve around personal fascinations, repetitive play behavior often merged into elaborate rituals corresponding to familiar routines in their daily lives. The children also began to explore and discover meaning in words and pictures. Echolalia and "echographia" (imitation of written words) took on more communicative functions in contexts associated with familiar routines and events. Primitive drawings began to take on crude yet realistic qualities, projecting images of people and familiar objects.

CHAPTER 8

Entering Play

IN MY SECOND year with Teresa, Freddy, and Jared, the school district relocated the "autistic program" to Loma Vista Elementary School. This school stood atop a hill in a working-class neighborhood, whose residents were mainly African American. The surrounding community struggled to overcome its dubious profile of high crime. Many families participated in organized efforts to support the school and community as a whole.

Close to half the students were African American, while the rest included a mixture from European, Asian, Latino, Middle Eastern, Eastern Indian, South Pacific Island, and Native American backgrounds. Approximately 30% of the students had what the district described as nonexistent or limited English proficiency. In addition to my class, there were two other special education classes on site, one of which was noted for its highly innovative and effective inclusion practices.

In this climate of diversity and social acceptance, Integrated Play Groups came to life. Teresa, Freddy, and Jared participated in two 30-minute play group sessions per week over a 2-year period. Each play group consisted of two novice players from my special education class and three expert players recruited from the general education classes.

In the first year, there were 11 children involved in four different play groups. Expert players included Carlos (8-year-old Latino male), Dina (8-year-old white female), Keila (9-year-old African American female), Misha (8-year-old African American female), Noah (9-year-old Latino male), Ronny (9-year-old African American male), and Sook (8-year-old Korean female). In addition to Teresa, Freddy, and Jared, a fourth novice player, Laura (10-year-old white female with autism), participated as well.

With Jane Goodall's patient and meticulous fieldwork with primates in their natural habitat as a model; I initially observed the children in their play groups for approximately 2 months before intervening. I provided no guidance other than telling the children that they were free to play with whomever and whatever they liked as long as they followed some basic rules: Stay in the play area, ask if you want or need something, treat each other with respect, and treat the toys with respect. This was a time to reflect upon how Teresa, Freddy, and Jared entered into the world of peer play.

SUBTLE ATTEMPTS TO PARTICIPATE

Teresa

From the very start, Teresa displayed a desire to be with her peers and attempted to join them in play activities. However, more often than not her attempts to engage another child or enter an established play situation went unnoticed. Relying on highly idiosyncratic strategies to initiate social interaction, she had difficulty clearly communicating her intentions. She spontaneously approached peers in a peculiar, naive, and one-sided fashion. For instance, she often repeated words, phrases, and even television commercials associated with a particular play activity. Moreover, she rarely oriented herself toward the other children while speaking. Teresa's inability to understand her peers' social perspectives often prevented her from being included in their activities.

> Teresa initiates dollhouse play with Sook while the other children organize materials to play grocery store. Standing beside Sook, Teresa touches and picks up the dollhouse. While pretending to vacuum, Sook momentarily watches her.
>
> TERESA: (*Facing dollhouse.*) Play in dollhouse, play in dollhouse. (*Briefly looks at Sook.*) Play in dollhouse, Sook?
> SOOK: (*Does not respond—stops vacuuming, briefly looks at basket of toys near the dollhouse, then joins the other children organizing grocery play.*)
> TERESA: (*Facing dollhouse.*) This is a dollhouse. Do not play in the dollhouse, do not play in the dollhouse. This is a dollhouse. (*Points to picture-word label on shelf.*) Says dollhouse. This is a dollhouse, dollhouse.

Teresa's physical proximity to Sook and repeated verbal and physical references to the dollhouse hinted of her interest in playing with Sook. Without a more definitive strategy, however, she failed to establish a shared reference to the dollhouse with Sook. Asking, "Play dollhouse, Sook?" was not direct enough to elicit a response from Sook, whose interest in the other children proved to be more powerful. On some level, Teresa seemed aware that Sook had forsaken her. She seemed to affirm to herself that she would not play dollhouse after all: "Do not play in the dollhouse." Unable to clarify her intentions and unaware that the other children had shifted activities, Teresa continued to fixate on the dollhouse.

Teresa frequently tried to enter established play situations with peers, but she lacked a sense of timing and an understanding of the subtle rules of social behavior. She essentially violated the rules of skillful play entry (she did not know how to approach her peers, hover and wait for a natural break, mimic and comment on their activities, or wait for an invitation). This often left her stranded in the midst of her peers.

> Teresa attempts to join Sook, Ronny, and Keila, who play grocery store with established roles of cashier and shoppers.

> TERESA: (*Walking to play grocery store.*) Come over here, OK? (*Facing away from peers.*) Easy checkout, easy checkout, easy checkout, easy checkout. (*Writes in air with finger.*) Easy checkout, you hear me? Easy checkout. (*Sees Keila pick up a pudding package, knocks on side of grocery store.*) You got any pudding?

> Peers do not respond; they continue to shop together. Teresa walks away from the grocery store.

Striving to join the grocery store play, Teresa abruptly entered the play situation by talking to herself—"Come over here, OK?"—and moving close to her peers. Rather than waiting for an invitation, she simply stepped into the play scene repeating a phrase from a television commercial for a local grocery store chain, "easy checkout." Repeating a commercial associated with grocery shopping indicated Teresa's awareness of the activity as well as her desire to join the play. While possibly familiar with this jingle, the other children did not decipher its meaning for Teresa. They continued to ignore her when she shifted her focus to a prop and asked, "You got some pudding?" In situations like this, Teresa simply gave up and abandoned the group.

Freddy

Freddy similarly demonstrated a strong desire to interact with play group members, but he repeatedly failed to establish a common focus in play with any of his peers, with the exception of his pal Jared. From the start, Jared engaged Freddy in reciprocal screams, face-to-face exploration, and physical affection. At first Freddy eagerly submitted to Jared's rather aggressive pursuit, but this quickly reverted into a ritual in which Freddy's responses were on automatic pilot. Devoid of any sense of pleasure, he attempted to break away from Jared's consuming ways and interact with the other children.

Freddy indirectly expressed his interest in his peers by watching their activities, playing beside them in the same play space, interacting with the same play materials, and imitating isolated play schemes. While he sporadically approached his peers to initiate activities or join an established play event, his attempts were generally roundabout and out of sync with the rest of the group.

> Freddy watches as Ronny, Keila, and Sook take turns hiding in the play refrigerator. I warn them that this is dangerous and advise them to play safely. A moment later, Freddy quietly squeezes into the refrigerator, closing the door on himself. Meanwhile, Ronny, Keila, and Sook engage in other activities while Teresa watches. Not until Freddy pokes his head around the refrigerator door do they notice him.

> KEILA: Freddy's in there.
> SOOK: Freddy, come out.
> RONNY: Oh, Freddy locks hisself in there.
> TERESA: Come outta there.

> Keila walks over to rescue Freddy, pulling him by the hand. Freddy crawls out of the play refrigerator, holding Keila's hand. He stands by himself in front of the mirror for some time. He then goes to the refrigerator and repeats his earlier act of hiding.

> TERESA: (*Discovers Freddy, dances in front of the refrigerator while singing.*) Doggy-doggy where's your bone, doggy-doggy where's your bone, doggy-doggy where's your bone. Go get in the jail.
> SOOK: (*Runs over to Freddy.*) No. (*Opens the door, pulls on Freddy, quietly calls him.*) Come out. Don't go in there, OK?

> Freddy crawls out with Sook's assistance, walks away, and sits alone on the bench.

Freddy expressed his interest in his peers by imitating their earlier game of hiding in the refrigerator. He signaled his desire for attention by poking his head around the door to see what the others were up to. They responded immediately, but not in a way that would redirect Freddy and include him in their activities. While Teresa's unusual response—"Go get in the jail"—was perhaps her own roundabout way of making this into a game, the others did not pick up on this. Instead, they ignored Teresa and treated Freddy as though he were a small child who needed help to get out of a predicament. At first Keila and Ronny called out in tattletale fashion, warning of Freddy's demise. Keila and Sook took on the caregiver role, coaxing Freddy to come out and reprimanding him when he disobeyed for a second time. Each time Freddy reentered the play group, he was left alone to fend for himself as the others organized activities together.

Hiding became one of Freddy's favorite methods for initiating play. Upon discovering the futility of this method for joining his peers, he learned that he could attract their attention by intruding upon their play and resisting their efforts to pacify him.

> Carlos, Ronny, and Noah play cops and robbers. They pretend Noah is the cashier; Ronny the police officer; and Carlos the robber who has just stolen money, groceries, and toys from the store. Jared focuses on Freddy as he watches this scenario. Ronny runs to get the money and grocery items stashed in the icebox and takes them to the store.
>
> Freddy imitates Ronny by walking to the refrigerator and picking up different grocery items. He taps his finger on a plastic lemon and bangs it to his chin while watching his peers. He momentarily looks up at Emily, the video camera person, and greets her in his high-pitched voice: "Em-i-wee!" Holding the lemon, he follows Ronny and Carlos, who are playing behind the grocery store with a hand puppet. Freddy touches the puppet and smiles. He then crouches down, crawls into the base of the store, and pushes it over with his body.
>
> CARLOS: (*Attempts to save the falling store, calling over to Noah.*) Hey, look what he's doing!
> NOAH: (*Joins Carlos to rescue the store—laughs as he grabs the store just as it is about to fall. He pulls on Freddy to get up.*) Come on, get up, come on.
>
> Freddy laughs but refuses to get up.
>
> NOAH: Oh my God, Freddy!

Carlos, Noah, and Ronny failed to recognize Freddy's initial attempt to join them in play when he imitated Ronny and later joined Carlos and

Noah behind the store. It wasn't until Freddy actually interrupted the event that they took notice of him. The threat of the store tumbling down on the group elicited immediate attention to remedy the problem. While to some degree Carlos and Noah appeared irritated with this disruption, they also found the situation to be humorous. Once Noah began laughing, Freddy realized the effect of his behavior on his peers by resisting their efforts to stop him from knocking the store over. This set the stage for Freddy to seek attention by taking on the role of the "bad boy" in subsequent sessions.

While Freddy occasionally approached the other children in a more positive and even affectionate manner (such as tickling Sook and Ronny), he more often provoked them with his habit of knocking over the grocery store, throwing toys, and sprawling out like a blob in the midst of their activities. It was as though he were calling out to his comrades, "See me, I'm here, play with me." The effect these behaviors had on his peers varied from one event to the next. At times they regarded him as cute, with the innocence of a small child, and sought to subdue his behavior by gently teasing or admonishing him. At other times they lost their patience with his bad boy pranks and reacted antisocially by yelling at, grabbing, and pushing him and ultimately banishing him from their activities. It got to the point that unless Freddy was pestering his peers or raising havoc, they all ignored him—with the exception of his faithful devotee, Jared. For example, on one occasion Freddy uncharacteristically began a play session by approaching Carlos and asking him directly to play: "What do you want to play with?" Carlos simply walked away, leaving Freddy standing alone with a fading smile.

Jared

During these preliminary sessions, Jared spent a great deal of his time alone in play groups, with the exception of an initial period in which he successfully engaged Freddy in rather long exchanges. These episodes resembled exploratory behavior one might observe between babies.

> Jared sits beside Freddy on the floor, lets out a scream, placing his forearm over Freddy's face. Freddy responds by screaming, smiling, and looking at Jared with raised eyebrows and touching his shoulder. Jared giggles excitedly, turning his whole body. He screams and places his arm over Freddy's mouth, muffling his ensuing cry. Jared again laughs excitedly, turning his whole body: "Hee, hee." He touches Freddy's face with both hands and giggles again, flapping his arms and flicking his fingers. This exchange goes on for several minutes—screaming, touching each other's faces, holding

each other, giggling with increasing excitement. Jared appears to be in sensory heaven, flapping, screeching, smiling, staring with wide-open eyes. Freddy grows tired and lies on the carpet. Leaning over Freddy, Jared touches his face and crawls on top of him. Together they scream loudly and roll around the play area. Noah calls over and warns them not to hurt each other. Ronny goes up to Jared, faces him, and places his finger over his mouth saying, "Shhh!" Jared imitates this gesture, but then screams, pulling on Freddy's head, instigating this ritual all over again.

Eventually, Freddy resisted Jared's persistent attempts to engage him in this ritual, leaving Jared frustrated but nevertheless determined to win Freddy back. He thus continued to follow Freddy, initiating screams and physical interaction whenever the opportunity arose.

Jared expressed an interest in the other children's play, particularly during sessions when Freddy was not present or was unresponsive to his whims. He was especially attracted to their activities involving elements of motion, rhythm, and repetition. Rough-and-tumble play was particularly appealing.

Jared watches Misha, Carlos, and Dina as they roll around on the floor, tickling each other and shouting with laughter. Jared smiles, jumps, claps, flaps his arms, turns, and jumps in circles. His excitement escalates as he runs up to the group and joins them on the floor. At this moment, Misha and Dina move and sit on the bench. Jared follows them and sidles up close to them, smiling while covering his ears and moving his head from side to side. Misha and Dina look at him and giggle. They then jump up and walk away. Jared stands up, watching them excitedly. He seems uncertain about what he should do. He walks over to the mirror, examines himself, touching his eyebrows and eyes, and then shifts his gaze back over to Misha, Dina, and Carlos. They begin to laugh loudly again. Jared repeats his ritual dance—jumping, clapping, flapping, and giggling loudly. He runs back and forth between his peers and me as I stand on the sidelines.

Jared's idiosyncratic use of nonverbal behavior to express his excitement and probable desire to join his peers went unnoticed. While the children were in no way perturbed by his unusual approaches, they also were in no way responsive. This left Jared in a state of frenzied uncertainty. Running to me was a sign of seeking some sort of clue, perhaps to make sense of all the commotion or find an outlet for his own energy.

Without direction, Jared characteristically remained alone in play groups, taking on the more passive role of watching his peers. Occasionally, another child would approach him to include him in an activity. Jared compliantly followed along for a moment or two but generally had little success in sustaining an interaction. On one rare occasion, Jared expressed an idea of his own.

Dina and Misha approach Jared, who sits alone on the bench. Dina bends over to his level and faces him.

DINA: Hi.
JARED: (*Looks at Dina, echoes.*) Hi.
DINA: (*Takes Jared's hand.*) Do you wanna play?
JARED: (*Accepts Dina's invitation, stands up while holding her hand, and responds.*) Want play group.
DINA: (*In an affectionate tone.*) What you wanna play?
JARED: (*Slowly states the title of a favorite book.*) Want—Happy— Birthday—Moon.
MISHA: (*Interrupts Jared, goes up to him.*) Come on, yeah let's play, you be in the kitchen.
JARED: (*Repeats.*) Want—Happy—Birthday—Moon, *want*—Happy— Birthday—Moon.

Misha and Dina organize groceries in the play kitchen, leaving Jared alone.

Jared's request to read a beloved book with his peers was a request he often made of me at the end of the school day following play groups. Without someone to interpret Jared's halting speech, Misha and Dina were clueless about what he possibly could be saying. Once again, Jared was deserted by his peers, left alone to amuse himself.

GRAVITATING TO RULES AND RITUALS

Teresa

Teresa's frequent exclusion from peer play activities resulted in her spending extended periods of time in isolation. She often wandered aimlessly as the other children played. To occupy herself, she created rituals within the confines of the play group. For instance, Teresa repeated the play group rules while admonishing Laura, who periodically failed to follow them.

Stay in the play area. Stay in the play area.
Did I ask you stay in the play area?
Stay in the play area.
What we doing right now? What we doing right now?
Stay in the play area.
What we doing right now?
Stay in the play area. Stay in the play area.

Teresa also instituted favorite classroom routines in her play group sessions, chanting as she performed them.

Got to dust. Got to dust.
Keep dusting. Keep dusting.
Got to dust. Got to dust.
Keep dusting. Dust. Keep dusting.
Dust, I tell you. Dust.

While performing her rituals and chanting, Teresa often watched the other children play. Although she seemed interested in their activities and materials, she only occasionally imitated them. Neither her solitary nor her parallel play resembled the play of her peers. Despite her earlier interest in dolls, she ignored them in these early play group sessions. On the rare occasions when Teresa spontaneously engaged in an activity, she contrived repetitive and unimaginative play themes with objects that fascinated her. For instance, she verbally commented on various makeup items while filling and emptying a purse.

I put my makeup in my purse. I got makeup.
I got makeup in there. My makeup. My lipstick.
Put my mirror in my purse. I put it right in my purse. Put it in your
     purse. Put it in your purse.
Put makeup in my purse.
I got makeup in there. I got makeup in there.

Constrained by the physical properties and features of realistic objects, Teresa was unable to elaborate or diversify her play themes. Although she understood the functions and relationships of objects—in this case, makeup and purse—she restricted their conventional use. For instance, Teresa filled her purse with apparent interest in each of the makeup items but never applied the makeup to her face. Her preoccupation with the ritual of naming each item as she filled the purse limited her ability to integrate novel actions.

Freddy

Similar to Teresa's, Freddy's repertoire of play activity consisted mainly of rituals based on earlier fascinations with materials. His preoccupation with spherical objects and commercial products motivated him to hoard the grocery items. He often rummaged through the box of groceries filled with replicas of fruits and vegetables and well-known packaged food, reading their labels and mouthing and tapping them and banging them to his chin. He frequently latched onto a product or plastic shape, keeping it under his arm while hiding and knocking the store over. At other times he dumped the box of groceries onto the floor and spread himself over them as though he were protecting his lot of jewels.

During periods of isolation, Freddy often wandered around the play area, exploring different materials.

> Holding an elastic headband in his hand, Freddy walks to the play stove and opens and shuts the oven door. He wanders over to the mirror, gazes at himself for a moment, then wanders to the toy shelf. He picks up the play telephone. While holding the base without placing the receiver to his ear, he randomly presses buttons. Freddy leaves the telephone and goes back to the mirror. He places the headband on his head hippie style. He takes it off his head and walks around the play area, holding, stretching, and eventually flinging the headband. Once again, Freddy goes to the mirror and gazes at himself.

Although Freddy mainly manipulated toys in a more or less stereotyped manner, he sometimes used them in conventional ways, thus indicating his understanding of the functions of objects. His functional play involved single and combined play schemes, such as rolling a car on the floor or pressing the keys on the cash register and retrieving money. On two occasions, Freddy displayed isolated symbolic play acts reflecting delayed imitation of familiar themes. In one case, Freddy appeared to imitate the camera person, Emily, as she looked at the group through her video camera.

> Freddy goes to the toy shelf and pulls out the toy camera. He sits in front of the full-length mirror. Holding the camera over his eye, he presses the button as though taking a picture of himself. He continues to look at himself through the camera, fixes his hair, smiles, and takes another picture. He then places the camera on

the floor. Still looking in the mirror, he touches the box of groceries beside him. He continues admiring himself, fixing his hair and inspecting his smile.

A similar episode involved Freddy's fascination with television. Using a Styrofoam frame, he imitated a play event I had earlier initiated with him. He first placed the frame over his face, and then over Ronny's face. He then made a gesture that signified turning a knob of a television. This isolated action, although imitative in nature, gave a hint of Freddy's emerging capacity for pretending and sharing another person's perspective.

Jared

Jared similarly devised rituals in play that revolved around a host of obsessions, including his attraction to Freddy and sensory-rich events. When Jared was not involved in his ritual dance of screaming, clapping, jumping, and spinning around in midair, he remained relatively passive. He often sat alone for extended periods of time, staring blankly at nothing in particular, holding his ears, vocalizing, and contorting his face. While sitting alone, he sometimes imitated a classmate's unusual habit of licking his finger and then rubbing his finger on his face.

Rarely did Jared spontaneously play with toys or props. He unconsciously fiddled with objects strategically placed in his vicinity, for example, turning the knob of the pencil sharpener, tossing a plastic fruit in the air and catching it, and banging the keys of the cash register. On a few occasions, he demonstrated the ability to play with toys in more functional ways, such as pushing the shopping cart, holding the telephone to his ear, and playing the toy record player. These types of play acts comprised only single schemes.

Spending a great deal of time alone and perhaps even bored, Jared often wandered around the play area searching for something to do that was familiar to him. He often focused on Laura, a classmate whose behavior he could easily predict.

Jared jumps around flapping, focusing on Laura, who crawls about on the floor. He follows and nudges her with his knee from behind. Poor Laura is obviously not enjoying this—she frantically chews her nails and approaches me. Jared follows, watching as I coax Laura back into the play area. Jared sticks close to Laura, imitating her as she chews on her nails. Laura chants the familiar words "Closing circle." Jared listens intently; his excitement intensifies. He jumps and spins wildly around the play area in his ritual dance, laughing and giggling while focused on Laura. He wanders to the other children, looks in at their play for an instant, then jumps back to Laura, nudging her along the floor until it is time to clean up.

At other times, Jared looked for activities involving reading and counting. Since he was not able to obtain his cherished books with the help of his playmates (books were not explicitly available in play groups), he read the labels and rules posted around the play area. He incorporated a counting theme in another ritual involving a familiar gesture that he routinely saw connected to himself whenever he screamed.

Jared stands before the free-standing, full-length mirror. Draping his arms over the top, he gazes at himself. Placing his hands on its sides, he vigorously shakes and rocks the mirror. He puts his index finger up to his lips in a shushing gesture making the *shhh* sound. He then changes hands, placing his other index finger over his mouth and counts, "One-two-three." He repeats this, alternating hands, repeating the *shhh* sound and counting, "One-two-three."

PROMISE OF BRIEF ENCOUNTERS

Teresa

By nature, communication is reciprocal, involving two-way interactions. Thus the isolation Teresa experienced in play groups stemmed not only from her own limitations but also from her playmates' dearth of skill and experience in interpreting her intentions. While Teresa's peers commonly disregarded her initiations, brief social exchanges occasionally transpired. As the children acknowledged and responded to Teresa, they unwittingly supported her advances in play.

Teresa watches Keila put groceries in the refrigerator as she pretends to be a mother while playing house.

Teresa: Can I have some soup, may I have some soup? (*Sings song from TV commercial.*) "Soup is good food."
Keila: No, no soup.
Teresa: Why?
Keila: Because.

TERESA: No more soup, may I have some soup? What we have for dinner today? Soup, we have soup. No soup. (*Sings from commercial.*) "Soup is good food." Put it the refrigerator. May I have some soup?

KEILA: No.

TERESA: May I have some soup, may I have some soup?

KEILA: No, no soup.

TERESA: Why? (*Laughing.*) May I have some ice cream?

KEILA: (*Laughing.*) No, no ice cream.

TERESA: (*Laughing even harder.*) Why? May I have some soup?

KEILA: (*Smiling.*) No soup.

TERESA: (*Laughing nearly uncontrollably.*) Why? Why?

Teresa and Keila clearly found pleasure in this shared event. As they took turns responding in a relatively predictable manner, a pattern of word play evolved. Interrupting this ritual with a novel event—in this case, replacing the phrase "May I have some soup?" with "May I have some ice cream?"—culminated in a brief exchange of laughter (although Teresa appeared to find this a lot funnier than Keila did). This playful interchange foreshadowed Teresa's emerging capacity for more spontaneous, flexible, and imaginative behavior. Although this interaction was relatively brief, it indicated Teresa's potential for coordinating and sustaining social play with another child.

Freddy

Freddy's encounters with his peers similarly held promise for future developments in play groups. Although he never sustained positive interactions with his peers for very long, many of the reciprocal exchanges that did transpire took on a quality of genuine affection. In many cases, Freddy was the instigator, sweetly calling his playmates or teasing them with pats and tickles.

Freddy watches as Keila plays with dress-up clothes. Sliding around on a pillow beside her, he turns to look up at her.

FREDDY: Keila.

KEILA: (*Smiles and looks at Freddy.*) Yeah.

Freddy tickles Keila under her arm, smiling.

KEILA: (*Affectionate voice.*) Hi, Freddy.

Freddy pulls Keila's head to him and embraces her.

KEILA: (*Continues in affectionate tone.*) Hi . . .

In another situation, Freddy gained attention by playing the bad boy with Ronny. This was perhaps the longest interaction that Freddy sustained with a peer during this initial phase of play groups.

Holding a ballet slipper, Freddy approaches Ronny while Ronny plays with toy cars. Smiling, Freddy lightly pats Ronny on his backside with the ballet slipper.

RONNY: (*Feigns pain.*) Ouch!

Freddy giggles and pats him again.

RONNY: Ouch!

Freddy giggles harder, patting him again.

RONNY: Ouch! (*Turns and looks at Freddy with an exaggerated look of surprise, holds his hands down to prevent him from hitting, and teasingly scolds.*) Bad boy Freddy.
FREDDY: Bad boy Freddy. (*Giggles, hits his own leg with slipper.*)
RONNY: (*Affectionately pats Freddy's leg.*) Bad boy, Freddy.

Freddy giggles, repeatedly hitting his own leg with the slipper. Ronny goes back to his car play. Freddy joins Ronny, takes a car, and rolls it on the floor.

RONNY: (*Grabs Freddy's slipper.*) Ha, ha, Freddy. (*Lightly pats Freddy on his backside with the slipper.*)

Freddy smiles and continues to roll the car on the floor.

This interchange resulted in mutual teasing, with Freddy and Ronny taking on reciprocal roles. By responding in kind to Freddy's unsolicited pats, Ronny naturally supported Freddy in extending this play interaction. Freddy imitated Ronny by patting himself and echoing, "Bad boy Freddy." His smiles and giggles indicated that he clearly understood that this was all in fun. Freddy also extended his play by following Ronny's lead when he reverted back to playing with the cars. At this point, Freddy played in parallel with Ronny, rolling a car beside him. He rarely initiated this type of play on his own. This example foreshadowed Freddy's capacity to socially coordinate and diversify his play with peers.

Jared

Jared experienced just a few brief social exchanges with peers. These were nevertheless precious moments, illustrating his potential for growth in play. While Jared typically failed to comprehend what his peers had in mind for him when they invited him to join a play event, on occasion they managed to reach out to him by communicating on a level he could more easily appreciate.

> Misha walks over to Jared and bends over to face him. She puts her face close to his and talks to him in a way that is familiar, the way an adult would approach a small child. Although I cannot hear Misha, she seems to extend an invitation to Jared to play. Jared moves his mouth in a way that makes me think he is echoing her words. She stretches her hand out to Jared. Jared complies by standing up and taking Misha's hand. Hand in hand, they walk together through the play area to the grocery store. As he passes me, Jared looks up with a genuine smile, a sight so rarely seen on his often emotionless face. With a sense of delight, he spontaneously shouts, "Play!"

At other times, Jared succeeded in focusing on play activities organized by his peers as they picked up on his subtle cues and diverted him from his usual rituals.

> Jared and Freddy stand watching as Noah, Carlos, and Ronny fool around and set up the play grocery store. Carlos approaches Jared with a puppet, holding it to his face.
>
> RONNY: (*Approaches Jared.*) What's my name?
> JARED: (*Echoes.*) Name.
> CARLOS: (*Egging him on.*) Noah, Noah.
> JARED: (*Echoes.*) Noah. (*Momentarily withdraws from Carlos and Ronny; approaches Freddy with a hug.*)

> Freddy reciprocates Jared's hug with a smile on his face.

> NOAH: (*Takes a puppet and approaches Jared, making it bark.*) Ruff, ruff.

Jared looks at the puppet quizzically, faces Freddy, and screams. Freddy reciprocates by screaming. Jared giggles, jumps up and down, and flaps his arms. Noah retrieves the shopping cart and pushes it beside Jared. Jared, in a hyper state, moves in Noah's proximity, looks at the shopping cart and at Noah.

NOAH: (*Acknowledges Jared by handing him the shopping cart.*) Here's the basket, Jared.

Jared takes the shopping cart and pushes it beside the grocery store, where Carlos, Ronny, and Freddy are situated. He then picks up the telephone attached to the store, holds it to his ear, and smiles.

FREDDY: (*Sits behind the store, mutters.*) Hello.

Jared hangs up the telephone. Still smiling, he walks over behind the store and tries to engage Freddy. Ronny pushes the shopping cart closer to the store. Jared leaves Freddy momentarily, retrieves the shopping cart, and offers it to Freddy.

By interpreting Jared's fleeting look as an expression of interest in the shopping cart, Noah unknowingly prompted him to take part in a joint play event. This simple response enabled Jared to break off from his recurrent ritual with Freddy. This activated Jared's exploration of play materials related to the play scene. His final offering of the shopping cart to Freddy was perhaps his own way of extending an invitation to join him in playing store.

INTERPRETIVE SUMMARY

Teresa, Freddy, and Jared's entry into Integrated Play Groups posed many challenges. They each communicated an interest in playing with peers. More often than not, their subtle and idiosyncratic social overtures went unnoticed by expert players, who busily engaged one another in mutual activity. Left alone and with little else to do, Teresa, Freddy, and Jared gravitated to rules and rituals known to them. They reverted to repetitive movement, activity, and elaborate routines centered around objects, people, and events in their immediate vicinity. On occasion, peers responded and supported Teresa, Freddy, and Jared in social exchanges. These brief encounters held out a promise for establishing interpersonal coordination and more complex forms of play.

CHAPTER 9

Guided Participation

AFTER APPROXIMATELY 2 months of observation, the second phase of Integrated Play Groups began. I supported Teresa, Freddy, and Jared through guided participation for a 2-month period (see Chapter 5). As a play guide, I focused on structuring opportunities for novice and expert players to coordinate play, while also challenging novice players to practice new and increasingly complex forms of play. This involved enticing the children to discover common ground on which they could collaborate in mutually enjoyed activities.

Observations of the often subtle and unconventional ways Teresa, Freddy, and Jared initiated peer interaction and play provided a context in which to recognize their potential. Similarly, observations of the expert players' intuitive abilities to involve and support Teresa, Freddy, and Jared in play events offered a starting point from which to begin structuring a system of support.

The idea of guided participation was to ensure that every child found her or his niche in the play group so as to form a collective whole. From my perspective, this required maintaining a global awareness of each child's behavior in relation to other play group participants in any number of different configurations. For instance, while directly guiding a pair of children, I remained cognizant of the activities of the other three children. The decision of when and to whom I provided assistance was based on an understanding of this dynamic process.

Monitoring play initiations was a critical part of the process. This involved recognizing, interpreting, and responding to Teresa, Freddy, and Jared's spontaneous play acts (conventional and unconventional) directed to self, objects, or peers. I considered these to be meaningful expressions indicative of each child's present and emerging social and symbolic capacities. Play initiations became the point of departure for novices and experts to participate in jointly constructed activities.

Scaffolding interactions were also a major part of the process. I found that I naturally modified my own behavior in response to the movement and patterns of the children's activity in play groups. Much of the time, I acted as an interpreter to help the expert and novice players figure out what the other meant by her or his words and actions. To start a play event, I sometimes directed the children and modeled social interaction and play as if the play group were a stage performance. I orchestrated play events by identifying common themes, arranging props, and assigning roles that ensured everyone a satisfying part. At other times I backed off and remained on the periphery of the group, giving verbal and visual guidance so that the children could set the stage for their own activities. I did this by posing leading questions; commenting on activities; offering suggestions; and giving subtle reminders, using verbal and visual cues with picture-word combinations.

Social communication guidance focused on promoting the children's use of conventional verbal and nonverbal communicative means to establish a common focus and coordinate play activities. I demonstrated ways to extend invitations to peers to play, persist in enlisting reluctant peers to play, respond to peers' cues and initiations in play, maintain and expand interactions with peers, and join peers in an established play event.

To guide social exchanges, I presented the children with simple logical sequences of nonverbal and verbal strategies. I also designed posters and corresponding cue cards depicting picture-word combinations of what the children can do and say to elicit and sustain another child's attention in play. Examples of nonverbal cues included the following: look (at playmate), stand close, tap shoulder, take hand, point, give (toy), and take turns. Examples of verbal cues included the following: say name (of playmate), then ask, Do you want to play? What do you want to play? What are you doing? May I play with you? Whose turn is it? May I have a turn?

Play guidance was another part of the process whereby I continually challenged Teresa, Freddy, and Jared to move beyond their present level of performance while immersed in playful activity. Play guidance involved fostering increased social coordination in play, moving from *orienting* (watching peers and activities), *parallel play* (playing side by side in the same play space with similar materials), and *joint focus* (active sharing, informal turn-taking in the same activity) to *joint action* (formal turn-taking), *role enactment* (portraying real-life activities through conventional actions), and *role-playing* (taking on pretend roles and creatively using objects while enacting complex scripts).

The following play scenarios illustrate the different layers of support provided to both expert and novice players through guided participation, as well as patterns of social interaction and play that emerged for Teresa, Freddy, and Jared.

TERESA'S EXPERIENCE

Dressing Up with Clothes and Makeup

Teresa's personal fascination with fashion made dressing up a logical activity for enhancing her participation in play groups.

Teresa watches as Laura, Keila, Misha, and Dina begin playing dress-up. Keila tries on a pair of shoes.

TERESA: Keila got big feet.
PAMELA: Teresa, what do you want to do?
TERESA: (*Walks over to Laura and zips up Laura's dress.*) I zip it, I zip it. Keep hands to self. Keep hands to self.
PAMELA: (*To Laura.*) She's zipping you up. (*Dina takes out makeup from the dress-up box.*)
TERESA: (*Looking at the makeup.*) Hi, Dina.
DINA: Hi.
TERESA: Can I see your purse? I got a sticker. (*Shows Dina a sticker on her hand.*)
PAMELA: Do you want to put on makeup?
TERESA: (*Jumps up excitedly.*) Put makeup on, you find me, you find me. (*Watches Keila as she puts on a dress.*) Button it up, button it up. (*Waving to Keila with both hands.*) Hi, Keila.
KEILA: Hi.
TERESA: It fit you, OK?
PAMELA: OK, who wants to play with the makeup?

Teresa raises her hand.

MISHA: Us!
DINA: Me!
PAMELA: Well, I think Laura and Teresa want to put makeup on, too. So could you all [play] together?
MISHA: Yeah.

DINA: Yes.

PAMELA: Remember, we talked about how to get [each other's] attention?

TERESA: Attention.

DINA: (*Walks up to Teresa.*) Do you want to put some makeup on?

TERESA: (*Smiles, nods her head.*) Yeah.

PAMELA: It looks like Laura's dressed up, Keila's dressed up, Dina's dressed up, and Misha's dressed up. Who's not dressed up?

MISHA: Uh, oh! You gotta get some clothes on, Teresa.

DINA: Get dressed, Teresa. Take those shoes off . . . and wear these.

TERESA: OK. (*Follows Dina's instructions, begins changing her shoes.*)

MISHA: Oh yeah, Teresa, put this shirt on . . . and wear these shoes.

TERESA: I copy a dress up. I put on shoes.

MISHA: (*Announces to group.*) They fit her!

TERESA: (*Excitedly.*) They fit you! I got big feet. Tie shoes.

MISHA: (*To Teresa.*) What size do you wear?

TERESA: Seven.

MISHA: Oh yeah, seven. (*Hands Teresa a dress.*) OK, Teresa, put this on. (*Puts the dress over Teresa's head.*) Put this on.

TERESA: (*Finishes putting the dress on herself, looking at her shoes and dress.*) They're fits you.

MISHA: They fit me.

TERESA: They fit me. (*Watches as the others begin putting makeup on.*) Keep your lipstick on, OK? I got lipstick.

MISHA: You want me to put this [makeup] on Teresa? You sit right here.

TERESA: (*Sits down, smiling.*) Hi.

MISHA: Hi. (*Applies makeup to Teresa's face.*) Oooh, look at your eyelashes!

TERESA: (*Giggles excitedly.*) I got makeup! (*Runs to Laura.*) Laura's got lipstick! Keep your lipstick on. Hi, Laura.

In this play scenario, Teresa initiated play with her peers in a roundabout fashion, watching and commenting on different aspects of the activity. As I modeled and offered suggestions to get the play event off the ground, the expert players responded to Teresa's subtle questions and comments, encouraging her to take a role in play. Gradually, I withdrew support, allowing Teresa's peers to direct her role in the play event. They initially gave her step-by-step instructions, pointing out what clothes to take and put on. Teresa actively followed their directions and expanded the interaction by eliciting comments relating herself to her peers. Eventually, Teresa achieved social coordination in play with Misha, engaging in joint action by taking turns exchanging play materials and brief remarks.

While in coordinated activity, Teresa displayed functional play by using realistic props in conventional ways.

Preparing Food with Play-Doh

Teresa's familiarity with food preparation in her daily life provided another context for her participation in social play activity.

> The children enter the play area. Teresa unloads a basket of groceries into the play refrigerator, while Freddy bangs on a piece of plastic fruit, Sook fools around with a timer by the stove, and Keila and Ronny dump miniature cars onto the floor. Pamela enters shortly after.

PAMELA: OK . . . now what did you guys decide on playing together?

RONNY: I want to play, ah . . . watchamucallit, ah . . . you know, that sticky stuff?

PAMELA: Play-Doh?

RONNY: Yeah, Play-Doh.

PAMELA: OK, is that something that everyone wants to play? Do Freddy, Teresa, and Sook want to play with it? Does Keila?

TERESA: (*Facing Sook.*) Wanna play kitchen? Wanna play kitchen?

SOOK: (*Taps Teresa's arm.*) Teresa . . .

TERESA: Play kitchen, I'll play kitchen.

PAMELA: OK, Teresa said she wants to play with the kitchen. Teresa, everyone else seems to want to play with the Play-Doh. Would you like to set up the table and have the Play-Doh?

TERESA: We eat, it time for dinner, time for dinner, dinnertime.

PAMELA: How about—if we get the Play-Doh we can pretend we're cooking?

FREDDY: Play-Doh. (*Raises his hand.*)

RONNY: Yeah.

TERESA: You cook, you cooking.

KEILA: I'm the mother.

PAMELA: (*To Sook and Ronny.*) Why don't you help move the table so people can sit down, and Freddy and I will get the Play-Doh.

Sook and Ronny set up the table, Keila examines the small stove, and Teresa unloads the grocery basket as Freddy helps bring the Play-Doh and tools to the table.

PAMELA: Here are some rolling pins; let's see what else you need, cookie cutters . . . Teresa, do you want to help bake some things?

TERESA: Bake a cake?

PAMELA: In the stove?

TERESA: Yeah.

PAMELA: (*To Teresa.*) Why don't you sit down with Keila and . . . (*To Keila.*) Why don't you go over and ask [Teresa]?

KEILA: Teresa . . . do you want to go play with this?

TERESA: Yeah. (*Without hesitation, walks over and takes a place at the table and begins playing with the Play-Doh.*). Play with Play-Doh. Wabby, wabby, wabby Play-Doh.

Keila follows Teresa and sits beside her.

TERESA: Hi, Keila.

KEILA: Hi.

TERESA: What is your name?

KEILA: Hi.

TERESA: Hi. (*To Pamela.*) I'll cook on stove, I'll cook it. Teresa cooking, Teresa cook.

KEILA: (*To Pamela.*) You know what I'd do if I didn't have one of these things (*referring to rolling pin*)? I'd go like this (*flattens Play-Doh with hands*).

PAMELA: (*Suggests.*) Why don't you show Teresa?

TERESA: (*Watching Keila.*) Gotta cook, gotta bake, Keila? Gotta cook.

KEILA: (*To Teresa.*) I'm making cookies.

TERESA: (*Teresa copies Keila, flattening the Play-Doh, announcing excitedly.*) I'm making cookies, too. We all making, we hope, we happy, we bake cookies. We put in oven, we put in oven right here. OK, Keila? I bake cookies, I bake it.

In this play session, Teresa initiated cooking in the play kitchen while her peers requested to play with Play-Doh. To establish a joint focus, I suggested combining the two activities into a common pretend play theme—baking. Verbally guiding the group and organizing materials for the activity, I arranged for the expert players to sit beside Teresa and model their play for her. Teresa gradually achieved social coordination in play with Keila as they engaged in joint action, sharing and taking turns with the Play-Doh. This eventually shifted to role-playing when Keila described to Teresa that she was baking cookies. Following Keila's lead, Teresa announced that she, too, was baking cookies. In this coordinated event, Teresa displayed the capacity for symbolic play by transforming Play-Doh into imaginary cookies and verbalizing her plan to bake them in the oven.

FREDDY'S EXPERIENCE

Shopping for Groceries

Freddy's fascination with grocery items made shopping a likely play theme for his participation in play groups.

> Freddy pushes the grocery cart. Ronny assists Freddy by lightly placing his hand on Freddy's back and guiding him to the grocery store. Keila takes the role of cashier; Sook and Teresa play customers. Freddy hands grocery items to Keila.

> KEILA: Wait a second. (*Gets a shopping bag and places grocery items in bag, then hands Freddy the play money.*)

Freddy looks at the play money, taps it, spreads it out, and fans it. Keila organizes her cashier area.

> PAMELA: OK, you're losing your customers.
> KEILA: OK, OK. (*Begins putting groceries in bag.*)
> PAMELA: (*To Freddy.*) Ask Keila, "How much?"
> FREDDY: (*Holding play money up to Keila.*) Money.
> PAMELA: Say, "How much?"
> FREDDY: Pay. (*Hands money to Keila.*)
> KEILA: Wait.

Freddy holds money out to Keila.

> KEILA: No, no, no, no, no . . . I didn't tell you how much it cost yet. (*Punches keys on cash register.*)
> RONNY: (*Assists Freddy by handing his grocery items to Keila as she punches in the keys.*) Come on, Freddy, Freddy, Freddy, come here.

Freddy gets into the rhythm of handing items to Keila.

> KEILA: The carrot's rotten; are you sure you want this carrot?
> RONNY: How much does it cost?

KEILA: Fifteen, it costs 11 dollars and 21 cents.

Freddy hands money to Keila.

KEILA: (*Gives Freddy change and hands him his bag of groceries.*)
Thanks for shopping at the supermarket.

At the start of this play scene, Freddy indicated an interest in shopping by pushing the shopping cart. Ronny spontaneously offered Freddy
his assistance by lightly guiding him in the direction of the grocery store.
This enabled Freddy to enter an established play event in which the other
players had taken on various roles. At this stage I stood by, allowing the
group to get organized and get started. Once Freddy made his way to the
grocery store, he seemed uncertain about what to do with the money Keila
(the cashier) handed him. At this point, I stepped in, verbally guiding the
different players and modeling ways to instruct Freddy in a simplified
manner. Ronny adjusted accordingly, modeling for Freddy how to give the
grocery items to Keila. Freddy eventually achieved social coordination in
play as he took turns with Keila, enacting the role of a customer (giving
her grocery items to ring up on the cash register and exchanging money).
At this point, Freddy displayed functional play in his use of play materials and enactment of conventional actions in a familiar activity.

Preparing Food with Play-Doh

Freddy's fascination with groceries and product names offered opportunities for his involvement in the familiar activity of food preparation.

Freddy sits beside Sook and Ronny at the table as they all play with
the Play-Doh.

PAMELA: (*To Freddy.*) What are you making?
FREDDY: Play-Doh.
PAMELA: You're making Play-Doh?
FREDDY: Pancakes. (*Pats Play-Doh.*)
PAMELA: Ask Sook what she's making.
FREDDY: Pancakes.
PAMELA: Say, Sook . . .
FREDDY: (*Repeats.*) Sook.
PAMELA: What are you making?
FREDDY: Making pancakes Play-Doh.
PAMELA: (*To Freddy.*) You're making pancakes?

FREDDY: Betty Crocker.
PAMELA: Betty Crocker pancakes?
FREDDY: Eggs. (*Flips pancake into the air.*) Eggs.
PAMELA: What is Ronny making?
FREDDY: Making Play-Doh.
SOOK: (*Quietly.*) Freddy, can you share your Play-Doh?

Freddy holds his pancake to his mouth, pretending to eat it.

SOOK: Freddy . . . (*Looks up at Pamela.*)
PAMELA: Do you want to listen to Sook?
FREDDY: Sook, make pancakes. (*Points to oven.*)
PAMELA: Sook asked you a question.
SOOK: Can I have some of your Play-Doh?
FREDDY: Oven.
PAMELA: Yes or no.
FREDDY: Yes, oven.
PAMELA: Tell Sook what you want.
FREDDY: I want oven.
PAMELA: You want to cook in the oven? (*Handing baking pan to Sook.*) Why don't you ask Freddy if he wants to use this?
SOOK: Freddy, Freddy, do you want to use this?
FREDDY: (*Takes pan, places it in oven, turns the knob, points to the oven.*) Oven, oven.
PAMELA: (*To Ronny.*) What's Freddy doing, Ronny? Do you want to ask him what he's doing?
RONNY: Freddy, Freddy, Freddy, Freddy, what are you making, Freddy, what are you making?
FREDDY: Oven.
RONNY: Oven? (*Giggles, looking at Pamela.*) He making oven.
PAMELA: Ask him again.
RONNY: Freddy, Freddy, Freddy, Freddy . . . What are you making?
FREDDY: Oven.
RONNY: Are you making cookies? Making cookies? (*Freddy begins making balls out of Play-Doh and throws them in the air.*) Freddy, Freddy, Freddy, Freddy, whatchu making?
FREDDY: Oven.
RONNY: Are you making cookies, are you making cookies?
FREDDY: Cookies. (*Points to oven.*)
RONNY: (*To Pamela.*) He making cookies.
FREDDY: (*To Pamela.*) Delicious, mmmm, delicious.
PAMELA: Tell Ronny.

FREDDY: Ronny, delicious, mmmm, delicious.
RONNY: Delicious?
SOOK: Mmmm, delicious.
FREDDY: (*Rolls up flattened Play-Doh.*) Taco, tomato, cheese. (*Pretends to eat it.*) Taco, taco, taco, taco, taco, mmmm, tomato, tomato.
SOOK: Is it good?
FREDDY: Mmmm, ahhhh!

In this play scene, the group began with a joint focus on playing with Play-Doh. To enhance social interaction and the diversification of Freddy's play, I modeled questions and redirected the players to exchange information about the play activity with each other by asking, "What are you making?" Throughout the process of questioning, including an attempt to clarify Sook's request to Freddy to share his Play-Doh with her, Freddy and his peers gradually achieved social coordination in their play. With coaching, Sook and Ronny persisted in their attempts to engage Freddy with questions. Freddy and his peers began to spontaneously take turns, exchange materials, and comment on the play. Within the context of this shared event, Freddy transformed his Play-Doh into an assortment of imaginary foods, displaying the capacity for symbolic play. In addition, he incorporated and combined novel schemes while pretending to prepare, cook, and eat the food he created.

JARED'S EXPERIENCE

Building and Knocking Down Blocks

Systematically building and knocking down blocks offered Jared both structure and excitement that appealed to his fascination with order and visual movement.

Noah sets up blocks on the floor. Jared follows Freddy under the table. Carlos calls and gestures to Jared and Freddy to come out from under the table.

CARLOS: Freddy, come on, come on. You too, Jared, come on, come on, come on. We're going to take turns.
PAMELA: (*Holding visual cue card—"LOOK."*) What do you need to do first?
FREDDY: (*Whispers.*) Look, look at me.

PAMELA: What are you going to say to Freddy and Jared?
CARLOS: OK, look, look, look at me.
NOAH: (*Hands Freddy a block.*) Put this on top. (*Freddy places block on top of row of blocks.*) Good boy.

Freddy starts to put another block on top.

CARLOS: What about Jared?
NOAH: I know, I know, Jared, put this on top.
CARLOS: (*Hands Jared a block.*) Put this on top, come over here, like this.

Jared places a block on the structure. Carlos claps. Jared claps.

NOAH: Now . . .
CARLOS: (*Looks at visual cue card—"WHOSE TURN IS IT?"*) Whose turn is it?
NOAH: (*Hands block to Freddy.*) Now, Freddy, Freddy, this is what I want you to put, put that right there. (*Freddy puts block on top.*) Good.

Jared moves closer to the structure.

NOAH: (*To Freddy.*) Now you got to wait your turn.
PAMELA: (*Holding visual cue card—"TAKE TURNS"*) Now ask, "Whose turn is it?"
FREDDY: Carlos.
NOAH: Good.
PAMELA: Good, yeah . . . Now think of some other things you can do and say.
NOAH: Now, Jared, come here. (*Jared puts block on structure.*) Good. (*The four boys continue taking turns, building the tower higher and higher; Jared loses focus.*) OK, Jared, this is what I want you to do. Get a block.
CARLOS: Block. (*Points to block, pulls Jared's hand.*) Block.
PAMELA: Say, "Pick up."
CARLOS: Pick up, pick up, pick up, pick up, pick up.

Jared picks up the block, places it on the tower; the tower begins to wobble. Freddy approaches the block tower with a devilish grin.

NOAH: (*Smiling.*) No . . . don't knock it down.
FREDDY: Whoops, whoops. (*Knocks the block tower over.*)

Jared jumps and laughs excitedly.

PAMELA: (*Teasing.*) What happened?
FREDDY: (*Looking at Pamela.*) It fell down, whoops.

In this play scene, I used verbal and visual guidance with cue cards to coach the players to look at each other and the play materials, take turns placing the blocks on top of one another, and praise each other. The expert players established a rhythm in which Jared shifted from joint focus to joint action while taking turns building with the blocks. Within the context of this coordinated event, Jared demonstrated functional play, using the blocks in a conventional manner. The final stage of knocking over the block tower introduced an element of novelty into this predictable activity to which Jared reacted with a rare sense of delight.

Connecting and Crashing Trains

Connecting and crashing trains similarly provided a structured format that appealed to Jared's fascination with order and movement.

> PAMELA: Right now I want you guys to try to remember some of
> the things we've been [talking about] . . .
> MISHA: Can we play dollhouse?
> CARLOS: Noooo!
> PAMELA: What I'd like you to do is ask [each other] what you'd like
> to do.
> CARLOS: (*To Jared.*) Do you want to play trains, trains?
> JARED: (*Echoes.*) Trains.
> CARLOS: Trains?
> JARED: Trains.
> CARLOS: OK, what do you wanna play? Say, "Trains."
> JARED: Trains.
> CARLOS: Do you wanna play trains?
> JARED: Trains.
> CARLOS: (*Silly voice.*) Na-nah-na.
> JARED: (*Echoes.*) Na-nah-na.
> CARLOS: Ma-ma-ma-ma-ma . . .
> JARED and CARLOS: (*Simultaneously.*) Ma-ma-ma-ma-ma . . .
> CARLOS: (*Points to shelf.*) Go get the train.

Jared goes to the shelf, picks up the train, and looks to Carlos for further guidance.

CARLOS: OK, get it out. (*Jared and Carlos together take the train off the shelf and place it between them on the bench. Carlos begins taking the train sections out of the basket; Jared watches.*) We're playing with the trains. OK, which one's going to be the first one, Jared, which one goes first?

Jared continues watching, begins to touch a section of the train, but withdraws his hand.

CARLOS: OK, do you want this one here? (*Holds a section of the train out to Jared.*)

Jared takes the train section.

CARLOS: Take it out, take it out, take it out, take it out. (*Carlos places it in Jared's hand, guides him to put it together with another section.*) OK, now you do it. (*Pointing to another section.*) Get that, get that, get that.

Jared picks up another section, looking for direction.

CARLOS: OK, do you want this piece too?

Jared puts it together with another piece.

CARLOS: Yea, Jared!!

Carlos continues instructing Jared. Jared starts to take more initiative in the play. He arranges pieces of the train. Jared notices the girls playing dolls; he stands up to take a look.

CARLOS: (*Gruff voice.*) Jared, get back here.
PAMELA: Oh, Carlos, do you treat your friends like that . . . roughly?
CARLOS: No . . . (*Explaining.*) He started to knock these down.
PAMELA: It sounded a little bit mean; we're trying to treat everyone with respect [one of the play group rules]. Are you putting the train together? Now is a good time for you guys to do what?
CARLOS: Take turns.
PAMELA: OK, so give [Jared] a chance to do what you're doing.

Jared and Carlos take turns putting the train together.

PAMELA: Good . . . I like the way you're taking turns.

Carlos and Jared finish putting the train together.

CARLOS: (*Instructs Jared.*) Now pull, pull, pull the train.

Jared rapidly pulls the train across the bench, crashes it into the wall, and looks at Carlos.

CARLOS: You crashed it again!

Jared looks up at Carlos, smiling, and claps.

CARLOS: (*Smiling.*) Yea!! (*Claps.*) Now you killed all the people . . . yea!! (*Claps.*)
JARED: (*Smiling, repeats.*) Yea!! (*Claps.*)
CARLOS: Now you killed all the fools—yea!! (*Claps.*)
JARED: Yea!! (*Claps and smiles.*)

In this play scene, I provided the group with periodic verbal reminders to establish a mutual focus in play activity and to adhere to the play group rules. Carlos initially engaged Jared by playfully teasing him in an exchange of echoing words and nonsense syllables. Carlos redirected Jared to the trains, instructing him step by step to connect the train. Jared followed Carlos's lead, shifting from a passive to more active participatory role, taking turns in the process of extending the train. Gradually, Carlos's style of instruction shifted from giving directions to questioning and commenting on the event of crashing the trains. Jared engaged in joint action while taking turns crashing the train, yelling, smiling, and clapping with Carlos. Within this socially coordinated play event, Jared displayed functional play by connecting and pushing the train in a conventional manner. Crashing the train appeared to elicit a response of pleasure and excitement similar to that of knocking over the block tower.

INTERPRETIVE SUMMARY

The preceding play scenarios illustrated the approach adopted for guided participation in Integrated Play Groups. I provided novice and expert players with different types of support, focusing on establishing a mutual interest and elaborating play events. During these sessions, the expert players, in individual ways, more actively sought to engage the novice players to use materials, take on roles, and coordinate their actions in jointly constructed play themes. They gradually demonstrated growing competence in mediating and coordinating play activities without my ongoing direct support.

Concurrently, Teresa, Freddy, and Jared demonstrated growing competence in their ability to attend to the play event as prompted by the structure the peers provided. They gradually shifted their attention away from me, no longer relying on physical, verbal, and visual cues to guide their actions. While making this shift, they each displayed more complex forms of play relative to unstructured play group sessions. To varying degrees, they each learned to coordinate their actions with peers and to produce more flexible and novel play schemes. Within the context of coordinated play events, Teresa and Freddy showed emerging capacities for symbolic play, and Jared for more functional play with objects.

Embracing Play

DURING THE FINAL phase of Integrated Play Groups, I temporarily withdrew myself and all visual supports (posters and cue cards) to reflect on the children's progress for a 2-month period. I informed the children that the play group rules still applied and that they were free to play with whomever and whatever they liked. I was interested in the group's experience—the extent to which novice and expert players would mediate their own play activities as practiced in the guided-participation phase. I also wondered about the novice players' experiences—whether Teresa, Freddy, and Jared's newly acquired social and symbolic capacities would continue to surface and unfold in play and other forms of creative activity— whether they would ever reach a point of fully embracing play.

ACCEPTANCE AND MEMBERSHIP

Teresa

As Integrated Play Groups continued, Teresa and her peers actively pursued one another for play. The expert players discovered meaning in Teresa's idiosyncratic behavior. They learned to interpret and respond to her subtle references to play events. They no longer perceived her rituals as peculiar and incorporated them into play scripts. For instance, "Easy checkout" became instituted as a communal chant while they played grocery store.

Teresa's social behavior and language were radically transformed. Her endless flow of echolalic phrases became less circumscribed, more socially directed, and more connected to the immediate play event. Although she continued to have difficulties with the nuances of play entry, she compensated by using socially referenced language. She frequently commented on her playmates' activities as a strategy for joining them. She put forth such questions as "What are we doing?" "What are we making?" and "Where are we going?" to express this desire. Teresa also adopted the use of such social amenities as "Excuse me" and "Can I play with you?" as means to join the other children.

> Teresa joins two of her peers playing dollhouse. Keila is in the role of "Mommy" and Ronny in the role of "Daddy." They pretend it is morning and place their dolls around the table in the living room.

> Teresa: Hi, Keila.
> Keila: Hi.
> Teresa: Do you want to play dollhouse?
> Keila: Yeah.
> Teresa: Can I play house, too? (*Takes a female doll, moves it to the kitchen, and pretends to cook.*) Time to eat breakfast, bacon and eggs, eat bacon and eggs.

> Teresa takes her doll to the dolls at the table in the living room and serves the family an imaginary breakfast. Keila takes out a car, after pretending to eat breakfast.

> Teresa: Where we going?
> Ronny: I need a car. I got to go to work.

> Keila and Ronny argue about whether it's morning or nighttime.

> Keila: (*In a bossy tone.*) Time to go to bed. Everybody's got to go to bed.
> Ronny: Now I got to go wash his face.
> Teresa: Time to go to bed, time to go to bed.

> Teresa puts her doll to bed and begins arranging the furniture and labeling each room in the dollhouse.

> Keila: Come on, y'all, you got to come to bed, it's nighttime.
> Teresa: It's nighttime. It's dark out here. It's nighttime.

Freddy

Without adult direction, Freddy distributed his time between parallel and socially coordinated play with peers. The expert players learned to interpret and respond to his rather idiosyncratic behaviors, indicative of his interest in them and their activities. For instance, while Freddy clearly knew the names of each play group member, he frequently initiated interactions by asking, "What is your name?" The children simply went along with him by replying and turning the question back on him. This question often set the stage for more extensive and elaborate interactions. The expert players learned to adjust their language, gestures, and facial expressions to a level that Freddy could easily comprehend. While on the surface they appeared to treat Freddy as a younger playmate, their methods were crucial for regulating his social attention and fostering active participation.

Peers often extended invitations and persisted in involving Freddy in their activities. They graciously accepted his old and newly acquired interests, incorporating them into multiple episodes of socially coordinated play. His fascination with grocery items, hiding under the table, knocking over blocks, tickling, and referring to himself as "baby me" transformed into a variety of social exchanges with conventional play themes enriched by his peers' imagination.

> Freddy sits beside Sook behind the grocery store. Teresa and Keila bring their crying babies to shop. Sook places her arm around Freddy's back. One by one, she holds up several different grocery items, asking, "What's this?" One by one Freddy responds with the correct label.

> SOOK: (*Hands Freddy plastic butter stick.*) Give this to Keila.
> FREDDY: (*Calls loudly.*) Keila.
> KEILA: (*From the other side of play area.*) Wait, I'm not done. I gotta get the bags for you.

> Freddy places the plastic butter stick in his mouth.

> SOOK: No, no, no, no, that's not for you.
> KEILA: (*Brings bags to Sook and Freddy.*) Here the bags.
> SOOK: (*Begins ringing up items on cash register; hands bag to Freddy.*) Freddy, put it like this, hold, no, no, no, no, Freddy, hold. (*Guides Freddy to open bag and place groceries inside; hands Freddy various items.*) Put this in here.

> Freddy puts the grocery items in the bag. Sook and Freddy coordinate their actions—Sook rings up the items on the cash register; Freddy places them in the bag until it is half full.

> SOOK: (*Referring to bag.*) Give this to Keila.

> Freddy begins to hand the bag to Keila.

> KEILA: I'm gonna need more groceries than that.

Sook and Freddy jointly fill the bag as Keila hands them new grocery items. A bit later, they engage in a tickle game, smiling face to face. Freddy tries to grab the cash register; Sook pushes his hand away, redirecting him to the grocery bag. Freddy next holds the grocery bag up for Keila.

SOOK: (*To Keila.*) Those kinds of things are in the mailbox.
KEILA: I need a new telephone and a mailbox.
FREDDY: (*On cue, picks up the telephone.*) Hello.
KEILA: Wait, I need more groceries (*Hands money to Sook and Freddy.*) Here. Telephone . . .
FREDDY: (*Picks up telephone.*) Hello. (*Puts phone receiver on Sook's ear, then hangs up.*)
SOOK: (*Gives cash register to Freddy.*) Freddy.
FREDDY: (*Presses keys, calls out to Emily [video operator].*) Emiwee, what is your name?
SOOK: (*Hands bag to Freddy.*) Freddy, give this to Keila, give this to Keila.

Freddy hands the bag to Keila.

KEILA: (*Taking bag.*) Thank you.
SOOK: Have a good day.

Jared

The children similarly interpreted and responded to Jared's spontaneous initiations and interests, supporting him in social play activity. Jared no longer clung to Freddy to the exclusion of all other activity. He at times remained relatively passive—watching, following, and playing quietly beside the other children. At other times he overtly approached his peers for guidance, assistance, and sharing a social event by verbalizing, using the same materials, or offering objects. He also still used a variety of non-verbal means such as proximity, atypical facial expressions, vocalizations, and physical touch to communicate his intentions and desires.

As with Freddy, the expert players adjusted their patterns of language and gesture to capture and sustain Jared's attention to them and their activities. Some of Jared's peers perfected the art of scaffolding by gradually moving from the use of direct physical prompts, to verbal and gesture cues, to only intermittent support through comments related to the play context. The children also incorporated Jared's fixations into a variety of social exchanges, with repetition and imitation as key ingredients. For instance, they easily incorporated his enchantment with the written word and numbers into grocery store play.

Carlos sits beside Jared. They momentarily watch as Laura, Dina, and Misha play with the dolls.

CARLOS: What do you want to play, Jared?
JARED: Want to play.
CARLOS: What do you want to play?
JARED: Want to play.
CARLOS: What do you want to play, Jared?
JARED: Play Jared.
CARLOS: Play.
JARED: Play.
CARLOS: What?
JARED: What.
CARLOS: (*Pauses, gets the cash register, and brings it to Jared.*) Do you want to play shopping?

Jared watches as Carlos fools around with the buttons on the cash register.

CARLOS: OK, what do you want to buy, Jared? (*Carlos brings groceries to Jared.*) OK, pick anything you want to buy, pick what you want to buy.

Jared takes the groceries from the box, handing them to Carlos one by one. Carlos rings each one up on the cash register. At one point, Jared smiles, vocalizes, and touches Carlos affectionately.

CARLOS: What else do you want, Jared?

Jared hands him another item.

CARLOS: OK, what else, Jared?
JARED: (*Hands another item.*)
CARLOS: (*Reading the label.*) You eat too much chicken, you know. Do you want Hamburger Helper?
JARED: (*Picks up Hamburger Helper, looks at the label, reads.*) Hamburger Helper. (*Hands it to Carlos.*)
CARLOS: What else do you want?
JARED: Milkbones (*Hands Carlos Milkbones box.*)
CARLOS: This? Oh, I think this is on sale. Do you want this?
JARED: (*Reads label on box.*) Animal crackers.
CARLOS: (*Points to box.*) What does it say?

JARED: Animal.
CARLOS: What's that say?
JARED: Crackers.
CARLOS: Good, Jared, we'll take that. That's all. Oh, do you want this?

Jared hands items to Carlos, one by one.

CARLOS: You're buying so much stuff, Jared. OK, a dollar forty for all these things.

Jared gets silly. He starts throwing the remaining groceries over Carlos's head, creating a pile beside him.

CARLOS: Now I'll charge you more for throwing groceries.
DINA: Be quiet because the baby is sleeping.
JARED: (*Looking inside the grocery basket.*) All gone.
CARLOS: Your change. (*Hands money to Jared.*) Your change, do you want it or do you want me to keep it?
JARED: Keep it.
CARLOS: Money, you want money, today you get one dollar.
JARED: (*Takes the money, examines it, reads aloud.*) One hundred dollars.
CARLOS: (*Points.*) What does that say?
JARED: One hundred dollars.
CARLOS: Yup, that's only your paycheck for today, Jared.

BUDDING FLOWERS OF PRETEND

Teresa

Teresa's capacity for symbolic play fully blossomed in the context of shared play events. Synchronizing her actions with those of the other children, she enacted roles in sociodramatic play scripts. She modified and extended formerly repetitive schemes into evolving play episodes. She discovered innovative uses for objects and transformed them in play. No longer relying on realistic replicas to represent an object, Teresa also invented imaginary props to support the play event.

Teresa's transition from a literal to a pretend mode burgeoned in her doll play. In a process initially orchestrated by her playmates, she developed an attachment to a particular baby doll. Preparing to take their baby dolls shopping, Sook and Keila encouraged Teresa to join them. After choosing a doll of her own, Teresa spontaneously announced, "This is a baby. This is a girl. The baby's name is Morrell." For the remainder of the play session, Teresa recited the actions she performed on the doll; "The baby go shopping . . . the baby take a nap . . . the baby get dressed for tennis." At the close of the play session, Teresa's attachment to this doll became apparent.

TERESA: Time to put Morrell away. Morrell be here tomorrow?
SOOK: Teresa, say good-bye to Morrell.
TERESA: Bye, Morrell, see you tomorrow.
KEILA: (*To her doll.*) Bye, baby.
TERESA: (*To Pamela.*) Morrell be here tomorrow?
PAMELA: That's right, Teresa; all the dolls will be here tomorrow, including Morrell.
KEILA: And Janees? [Referring to the doll with which she had played.]
PAMELA: And Janees, too.

In their next play group session together, Teresa and Keila picked up where they had left off, each with her respective doll, Morrell or Janees.

KEILA: (*To Teresa.*) See, this is your baby.
TERESA: (*Smiles and simulates a familiar version of peekaboo with her doll.*) Find you, find you, you find me. This is my baby. (*Gazes at the doll's face and gently brushes the hair from its eyes.*) Hi, baby, hi, baby.

Appreciating this newly formed alliance, the expert players naturally incorporated Teresa and her baby in their sociodramatic play scripts. Within this social arena, Teresa explored multiple roles and realities in play. Modeling her peers, she approximated make-believe actions with her doll. The uncanny perfection with which Teresa initially mirrored her peers in play was reminiscent of her echolalic parodies. Teresa's "echoplaylia" transformed into flexible and spontaneous expressions in play in ways that paralleled the progression of her language from echolalic utterances to meaningful expressions.

The children pretend to go grocery shopping.

KEILA: (*Simulates crying with her doll.*) Waaa, waaa.
TERESA: (*Holding her doll.*) Waaa, waaa.
KEILA: Waaa, waaa.

TERESA: Waaa, waaa . . . We can help you? We can help you?
TERESA AND KEILA: (*In unison.*) Waaa, waaa.
TERESA: (*Holds doll with extended arms.*) Waaa, waaa . . . Morrell's crying, waaa, waaa . . . I can't find my mommy, I can't find my mommy. (*Brings baby close, looks at doll's face, with a sympathetic voice.*) Baby . . . you OK? (*Looking at Keila.*) Baby crying, Keila?
KEILA: Yeah
TERESA: Yeah. Morrell crying?

In the preceding scenario, Teresa initially emulated her playmate's doll enactment by animating the doll with physical sensation and emotion. While simulating a crying baby, she independently constructed an imaginary play theme. Enacting the separation and reunion of Mommy and Morrell, Teresa portrayed reciprocal roles of a frightened child and concerned mother.

Relying less on models for pretend play, Teresa's independent play scripts evolved. She increasingly used language and gesture to represent objects, people, and events. Although remaining bound to realistic themes, she developed an extensive play repertoire expanding on familiar routines and rituals. While playing house, Teresa organized groceries, cooked meals, dusted furniture, and cared for her baby. Complaining about her fidgety and whiny baby, Teresa held imaginary telephone conversations with her grandmother. Pretending to go grocery shopping, Teresa put on makeup and carried a purse filled with play money. While planning and coordinating multiple events, Teresa composed relatively complex and coherent play scripts.

In one episode, Teresa pretended to be a mother taking her baby to the bathroom while shopping. She enacted every detail, complete with sound effects.

(*Make-believe crying.*) Waaa! Waaa! Morrell is crying, waaa. Morrell is crying. You OK, Morrell? (*Puts baby doll on counter, pulls pants down as though checking for a wet diaper, makes baby jump up and down on her lap.*) You got to go to the bathroom, Morrell? Time to go pee-pee, right now, time to go pee-pee . . . That's right, time to go pee-pee, Morrell. You gotta go to the bathroom? . . . Go to the bathroom. Pull a pants down (*Pulls doll's pants down.*) Pee. (*Seats doll on make-believe toilet.*) Sssss. Pull a pants up (*Pulls doll's pants up; makes doll flush toilet.*) Pshh. You went to the bathroom, you went, we all went, you went to the bathroom, you went. You gotta put you shirt in the pants, right now. (*Tucks doll's shirt in pants.*) Put a shirt in the pant, pull pants up, you hear me? (*Pulls pants up.*) Pull up, pull up, you all tucked in right now, all tucked in, put a shirt in the pants, tuck in. You went to the bathroom, you went, Morrell.

Freddy

Although Freddy did not spontaneously present a full capacity for advanced pretend, he consistently exhibited functional play and other complex play behaviors indicative of emergent symbolism. He occasionally manipulated materials by picking up and inspecting different objects, pulling on levers, dumping groceries into a box, and building up and knocking over blocks. But these were isolated acts; he no longer engaged in uninterrupted rituals. In fact, Freddy ceased banging objects to his chin and only sporadically screamed in response to Jared's initiations.

Freddy clearly demonstrated his knowledge of conventional uses and relationships of objects through repeated displays in functional play and other more advanced forms of play. Many of his play acts involved combining more than one scheme using realistic replicas. For instance, he set up miniature traffic signs on the floor and moved toy cars around them. He demonstrated the function of various tools while engaged in a construction theme. He pushed a shopping cart, loaded it with groceries, and took it to the grocery store stand. Freddy not only acted on objects; he also directed play acts to himself and to other agents. He extended familiar play schemes to his peers.

> Freddy sits beside Sook behind the grocery store. Sook hands the telephone to Freddy.
>
> FREDDY: (*Holds phone to his ear.*) Hello. (*Pretends to dial.*) Hello. (*Places phone on Sook's ear.*)
> SOOK: Hello. (*Listens for a moment; hands phone back to Freddy.*)
> FREDDY: (*Holds phone to ear.*) Bye-bye. (*Hangs up phone.*)

He also reenacted familiar play schemes with dolls:

> Freddy places a doll in the doll bed and sets it on the floor beside Carlos.
>
> FREDDY: (*Looks up, smiles, and points to a doll lying on the bed.*) Baby, baby. (*Picks up doll, looks at it for a moment, touches its dress, explores under dress, looks back up.*) Baby me.
> CARLOS: (*Looks at Freddy, teasingly.*) Noooo! Are you a baby?
> FREDDY: (*Looks at Carlos, picks up doll, holds it to his chest, hugs the*

> *doll, pats its back.*) Baby. (*Places baby in the doll bed, gazes into doll's face while leaning over the bed, picks up the doll, holds it to chest, hugs the doll tightly, kisses the doll, gently rubs its head, smiles.*) Nice and soft, nice.

In another play session, Freddy connected this "baby" play scheme to a doll, Jared, and himself.

Freddy sits beside Jared on the floor.

FREDDY: (*Points to himself.*) Baby me. (*Gets up and walks over to toy shelf.*)

Jared follows Freddy.

FREDDY: (*Picks up a baby doll, hugs the doll to his chest, and points to the doll.*) Baby, baby.

Freddy looks into Jared's eyes, hands Jared the baby doll, placing it in his arms, presses the doll to Jared's chest, hugging both the doll and Jared. Jared reciprocates, hugging the doll and Freddy for just a brief moment. He hands the doll back to Freddy.

FREDDY: (*Smiles, takes the doll back, looks at the doll, rubs its arm.*) Nice and soft. (*Puts the doll back under the covers in the bed; momentarily greets Emily.*) Em-i-wee. (*Momentarily helps to clean up; goes back to the doll.*) Baby me. (*Picks the doll up, hugs it, looks at it, rubs its arm.*) Nice and soft, nice and soft. (*Places the doll on bed on toy shelf, faces Pamela and points to himself, smiling.*) Baby me.

Freddy also displayed a variety of isolated symbolic play acts similar to those exhibited in the guided participation phase. He was particularly fond of pretending to cook, using Play-Doh, and he created feasts of tacos, burritos, spaghetti, pizza, Hamburger Helper, cookies, and pancakes. He enacted gestures and sounds for specific acts such as a hand-twisting motion to signify turning on the stove, yelling, "Ouch, it's hot!" while touching the stove, and making slurping sounds and saying, "Mmmm, ahhhh, delicious," while holding Play-Doh up to his mouth. He also transformed a plain yellow bottle into a pretend object, referring to it as "Crisco oil." Shopping was another frequent play event in which Freddy took on various roles, as cashier, bag boy, shopper, and even one of the kids who received an allowance to buy candy and toys. While these symbolic play acts typically took place while he participated in socio-dramatic play, they sometimes were manifested as delayed imitation. In such cases, Freddy acted out pretend play in independent play activity that he had earlier witnessed while playing with peers, a form of delayed "echoplaylia."

Jared

Jared similarly presented more diversity in his play repertoire, with fewer stereotyped play acts and more exploratory and conventional forms of play. His increased participation in social play seemed to correspond to fewer incidents of highly ritualized responses to his environment. Jared's impulse to scream decreased, since now Freddy seldom reinforced him, and he now joined in rough-and-rowdy play rather than remain an energized by-stander. He began to explore objects in more typical ways—for instance, taking apart and putting together a toy train, pushing the ladder on the fire truck up and down, emptying and filling a box with play groceries, and building up and knocking down a tower of blocks.

Jared also exhibited spontaneous functional play, demonstrating his understanding of the ordinary uses and associations of objects. These play acts transpired in conjunction with activities organized by his peers. Jared rarely sought out play materials on his own but rather relied on peers to place them in his general vicinity. He mainly directed functional play acts to realistic replicas. He enacted a variety of single-scheme events similar to those exhibited during the guided participation phase, including moving toy cars across the floor, pulling a toy train, placing pots and pans on the stove, pushing a shopping cart, loading play groceries into a shopping cart, putting money in a cash register, and holding a toy telephone to his ear.

In a few instances, Jared spontaneously directed play acts to himself and other agents that were characteristic of simple pretense. In these cases, he typically enacted familiar events involving single schemes or combining more than one scheme. Unlike either Teresa or Freddy, Jared had not previously exhibited this capacity during adult-structured sessions. It is quite possible that these play acts represented delayed imitation of his peers, indicating that he still very much remained in a literal mode. As isolated episodes, they are nevertheless noteworthy. In one incident, Jared held a brief conversation on a play telephone, listening and responding with unexpected interest and pleasure.

> NOAH: Rrrring, rrring—hello—is anybody here named Jared?
> (*Calls.*) Jared, Jared.

CARLOS: (*Puts his hand out to Jared.*) Come on, come on. (*Jared takes his hand, walks over to Noah.*)
JARED: (*Jared takes the phone, holds it to his ear.*) Hello. (*Jared continues to hold the phone to his ear and switches ears while listening.*)
CARLOS: (*In a Grover-type voice.*) Hello, it's me, Jared, it's me.

Jared tries to place the phone on Carlos's ear as he talks.

CARLOS: (*Pushes the phone back to Jared, saying in Grover voice*) OK, Jared, do you want to come to Sesame Street?
JARED: (*Smiles brightly.*) Sesame Street, yes.
CARLOS: Yes?
JARED: (*Still smiling.*) OK.

Noah takes the phone back from Jared.

In another incident, Jared generalized the concept of baby to a doll, treating the doll as if it were a baby:

The boys play house and store with Ronny, Jared, and Freddy in the role of the sons who just bought a bag of toys with their allowance. Ronny pulls out a toy and hands the bag to Freddy. Jared watches as Freddy retrieves a doll.

JARED: Doll.

Freddy hugs the doll. Jared touches Freddy as he kisses the doll. Freddy holds the doll in a lower position.

JARED: (*Pats the doll on the head.*) Baby.
FREDDY: Baby.

Jared pats the doll on the head again. Freddy pats the doll on the head.

CONVEYING MEANING IN WORDS AND PICTURES

Teresa

As Teresa's pretend play flourished, she showed comparable achievements in other modes of symbolic activity, including her spoken language, writing, and drawing. Supported by an enhanced ability to express herself verbally, her make-believe play matured. While pretending with the other children and her doll, she used language in increasingly flexible and organized ways. She used a greater variety of linguistic forms to create integrated and cohesive play scripts. In addition, she combined language and gesture to represent imaginary events in play.

Teresa's expressions in writing paralleled advances in symbolic play and spoken language. She became a voracious reader and was particularly fond of reading books aloud to her classmates and her doll. During play group sessions, she naturally incorporated writing into her pretend play activities—for instance, she wrote imaginary notes to her bus driver while pretending to play school and created make-believe bank checks while pretending to go grocery shopping (see Figures 10.1 and 10.2).

The narrative structure of Teresa's writing was nearly identical to that of her speech. As was common in her pretend play, she often recounted familiar activities and events in her daily life. In the following writing example, Teresa recalled what she had done over her summer vacation. She appeared to playfully experiment with punctuation by inserting commas and periods in a seemingly purposeful fashion.

My Summer Vacation

My. Summer Vacation i Stay home, and watch tv Oprah and, Donaue. and news i watch the yound in Restless. i watch Loving. and tv. i stayed home with nana i make cookies with Nana oatmeal

Figure 10.1. Make-Believe Note to Bus Driver Created in Play Groups (Teresa, Age 9)

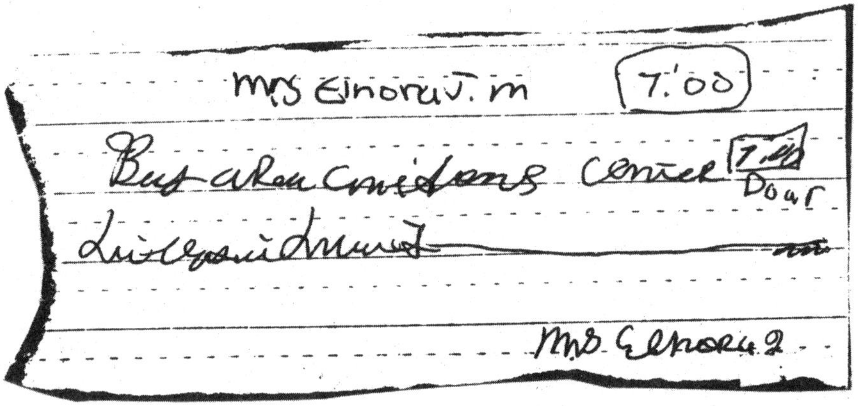

Figure 10.2. Make-Believe Bank Check Created
in Play Groups (Teresa, Age 9)

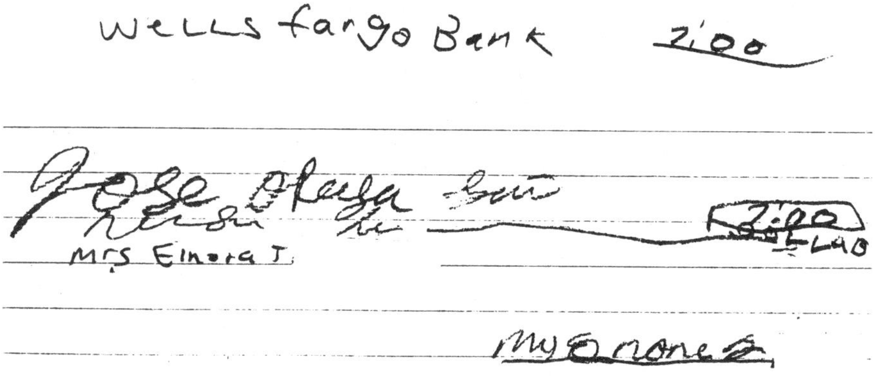

cookies, i washed dishes at home i played outside. i played jump,
rope, at, home. i played Ball at outside i wacted Mapletown, i
wacted Kaers Bear at home, i played Doll's i watched all my children and one Lik to Live. i watched Oprah and Donaue and the,
new's. i go eat Dinner at home, i cooking, at home. i have a cookout,
at outside. Nana was cooking, i got go in side the house' nana went
to Safeway buy, some food, Nana went home. with [uncles' names],
Teresa. i clean the Bathroom at home with Nana, i had a. fun
Summer. i played, my, cat, at home.

Teresa's writing grew to be more storylike. While included in a fourth/
fifth-grade classroom, she cultivated her writing skills in a cooperative
learning group. Assisted by some of her girlfriends from play groups, she
wrote and illustrated a story recounting a personal experience she had had
the previous year while visiting the city aquarium.

Dora the Star Fish

Dora swims in the water
She Lives in the Aquarium
Dora's Best friends are Boys and girls
They visit Dora everyday
One day Teresa went to Visit Dora the Star fish
Teresa got scared and was crying and Screaming
Dora said, Don't be scared I will be Your friend

Teresa is not Afraid anymore
She feels happy
the End

Teresa's drawings progressed in a fashion similar to that of her pretend play, spoken language, and writing. Incorporating rich detail, she represented familiar people, scenes, and events from her daily life. Her self-portraits grew to be more realistic, with distinct characteristics and features representing her African American identity. Plate 5 shows a picture she drew to represent what she would like to be when she grows up. The way in which Teresa constructed this picture was unique, as she first drew the fingernails (three on each hand), next the belly-button, and thereafter the face and body.

Plate 6 shows a picture of her home and family members. She carefully included such details as five fingers on each hand, particular hairstyles, clothing styles, and even facial hair in the case of one relative. She also attempted a three-dimensional rendering of her house with a three-quarter-view perspective detailing the roof with shingles. This type of house became a standard in many of Teresa's drawings.

Plate 7 corresponds to pages from her story "Dora the Star Fish," in which she included significant detail in scenery and characters. The children in her story have not only elaborate clothing styles but also rich, emotional expression on their faces.

Freddy

While Freddy also produced more complex and flexible forms of spoken language than was evident prior to the guided-participation phase in play groups, he was more consistent in generating novel phrases and sentences when guided by an adult in joint play scripts with peers. With his peers he tended to echo single words and simple phrases or to repeat stored phrases in association with certain events—for instance, by asking his peers, "What is your name?" or commenting on play materials by naming various products (such as "Crisco oil"). One might speculate that Freddy's peers placed less of a demand on him to produce language in play than I did as his teacher. He was, after all, able to participate in joint play activities using minimal language by simply taking a role and enacting the part with action and gesture. On the other hand, this limited his capacity to produce more imaginative and creative forms of play of the sort we saw Teresa develop.

Freddy similarly advanced in his written expression. He kept a journal and used a simple word-processing computer program to describe feelings and familiar events relating to the past, present, and future. Without specific guidance, he typically wrote single words or phrases corresponding to particular interests and events. For instance, he wrote the names of famous land-marks in San Francisco while looking at a pop-up book. He also spontane-ously labeled his drawings with people's names and features or objects he associated with them—for instance, he drew a picture of his instructional assistant wearing glasses and labeled it with her name and the word "glasses."

Freddy also demonstrated the capacity to write in complete sentences when prompted by an adult. In such cases, he effectively wrote what he initiated in a social conversation with an adult coaching him to repeat a spoken sentence and to put down each word as he spoke.

PAMELA: Hey, Freddy, what did you do this weekend?
FREDDY: Safeway shopping.
PAMELA: You went shopping at Safeway?
FREDDY: Yes.
PAMELA: Can you tell me again, I went . . . ?
FREDDY: I (*pause*) went (*pause*) shopping Safeway.
PAMELA: Who did you go with?
FREDDY: Papa.
PAMELA: Can you tell me again, I went with . . .
FREDDY: I went with (*pause*) Papa.
PAMELA: Can you write that down? I-went-shopping-at-Safeway.

Freddy writes as he repeats each word.

PAMELA: (*Continues.*) I-went-with-Papa.

Freddy continues to write as he repeats each word.

Freddy also wrote a story while included in a fourth/fifth-grade class during which he participated in a cooperative learning group. Assisted by his peers, he wrote and illustrated a story about a whale he named Alka Selzer. Freddy thought this name to be quite funny, since he was particu-larly fond of product names. The humor in this derives from his under-standing that whales and other sea creatures produce bubbles under water in a way that is similar to the fizz that comes from dropping antacid such as Alka Selzer in water.

Alka Selzer the Whale

To Mama and Papa
Alka Selzer the Whale
The whale is in the water

The whale's name is Alka Selzer
He swims with a school of fish
Alka Selzer visits Carlos
Alka Selzer goes to the aquarium and sees the star fish, alligators,
    and seals.
The whale feels happy
The end

Freddy's creative expression in drawing followed a similar pattern as that in his play, spoken language, and writing. He spontaneously depicted themes reflecting his personal interests and fascinations with objects, events, and people in his everyday life. Although he still used a somewhat primitive and ritualized style in his drawings, he experimented with different colors and forms through different media. He gradually included more detail and a greater variety of different elements to depict conventional themes. Moreover, he portrayed a greater variety of themes influenced by social experiences with peers and significant adults at home and school. While not decidedly imaginative in nature, his drawings progressively reflected his connection to the social world.

While in play groups, Freddy drew pictures beside his peers, representing themes typical of children's drawings in his age group (see Plate 8). He depicted Emily, the video camera operator in play groups, as he saw her with camera and tripod (see Plate 9). He generated numerous self-portraits, portraying himself with his family (see Plate 10) and involved in various activities and events—such as playing the drums (see Figure 10.3), having a picnic (see Plate 11), and going ice skating (see Plate 12).

Jared

Although Jared's language did not significantly improve from the time he began play groups, there were quantitative and qualitative changes worth noting. Specifically, he more consistently echoed his peers by repeating single words, phrases, and parts of sentences. Rather than simply parroting his peers without intention, his echolalic utterances were more communicative in nature, comprising responses, requests, and comments. For instance, to join his peers in a derivation of hide-and-seek, Jared followed a peer who hid under the table and yelled, "Boo," a word he had heard earlier in connection with this game. Jared also spontaneously commented on objects and events in play, saying, "All gone," when he completed emptying a box; "Up, up," while pointing to the word "up" in a pop-up picture book he read with Carlos; and "Doll," and "Baby," while interacting with Freddy and a baby doll.

Figure 10.3. Self-Portrait with Drums in Water-Base Marker (Freddy, Age 9)

While Jared's written expression paralleled his speech development in terms of its imitative and rote quality, his writing also changed in ways that were not comparable to his speech. He no longer perseverated in his writing by repeating the same symbol or word without variation. Instead, he spontaneously reproduced written information memorized from books, worksheets, classroom charts, and schedules, similar to the way Teresa had first initiated writing. He particularly liked to write on the chalkboard, erasing and replacing information in his own handwriting. On the computer, he typically rewrote familiar information such as his name and address or the days of the month.

With adult assistance, Jared also kept a daily journal, writing simple phrases and sentences to describe events, feelings, and experiences. Through frequent probing, he expanded and integrated rote responses to questions about familiar events and routines.

I watch birds Recess birds Fly in the sky I like birds birds

Jared is weArG glasses

MyAfternoon
Ieatlunch
AftersIdoschoolwork
IgotoPlayGroup
Itakethebushome

Jared's expressiveness in drawing and painting surpassed that of all other symbolic activity, including his spoken language, play, and writing. As was true in his spontaneous writing, he no longer restricted his drawings to repetitive and unwavering themes. Although many of his drawings retained a somewhat imitative and ritualized style, he depicted realistic and conventional themes relating to personal interests and experiences. Adhering to single themes, he represented physical features of his environment and himself with a certain degree of accuracy.

Inspired by his great fondness for technology, he produced a rather detailed and colorful rendering of a computer. Following a trip to the aquarium, he drew a sea creature submerged in water with waves and a grassy shore in the background (see Figure 10.4). This was by far his most advanced drawing in terms of visual perspective.

Figure 10.4. Sea Creature in Water-Base Marker (Jared, Age 10)

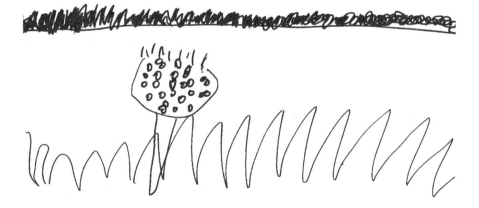

Jared's self-portraits were at first rather stereotypic, but gradually took on more realistic proportions and features. Initially he seemed content with quickly getting the picture on paper and forgetting about the details, particularly when he drew pictures in his journal (see Figure 10.5). He later paid particular attention to detail, making sure to include visible features of the human face and body (see Figure 10.6). Jared's most dramatic

Figure 10.5. Self-Portrait with Teacher in Pencil (Jared, Age 9)

Figure 10.6. Self-Portrait in Crayon (Jared, Age 10)

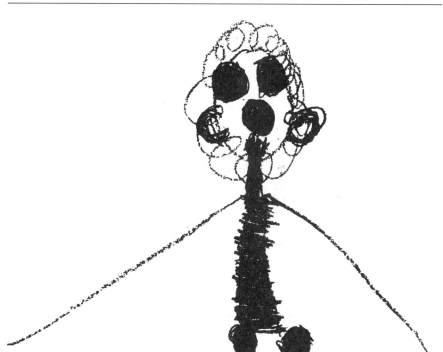

self-portrait showed him ice-skating, an activity he greatly enjoyed. He included not only all the paraphernalia necessary for ice-skating, but also a smile on his face to express his pleasure (see Figure 10.7).

INTERPRETIVE SUMMARY

Teresa, Freddy, and Jared each embraced play in its many forms. They became accepted as fully functioning members of Integrated Play Groups, participating with various players in a variety of events. They were no longer perceived as bizarre or peculiar; their unique fascinations were assimilated into conventional activity; and, in some cases, group members adopted these as the norm. Within the realm of shared experiences, each child displayed more complex forms of play. These surfaced in different ways, appearing as "echoplaylia" (imitation of play acts) and simple pre-

Figure 10.7. Self-Portrait Ice-Skating in Pencil and Crayon (Jared, Age 10)

tend (realistic role enactment) and, in Teresa's case, fully blossomed into advanced pretend in which she transformed and invented objects, dolls, and roles in play. These budding flowers of imagination similarly surfaced in the children's growing capacities to convey meaning through verbal and visual images in stories and pictures.

C H A P T E R   1 1

An Unending Journey

SPREAD BEFORE ME are the many photographs of Teresa, Freddy, and Jared I have collected over the years. As I gaze into their sweet faces I feel moved by the many moments we had together, unable to fathom that they are no longer children. Looking back, I recall our last weeks together at Loma Vista as Teresa, Freddy, and Jared prepared to go on to higher grades in new schools. There were many activities that revolved around their graduation, a symbol of moving on to new beginnings. As these children accumulated new experiences with people, places, and things in their world, I wondered what they took with them from the past. What has become of their memories and achievements in Integrated Play Groups? How have their social and imaginary worlds been transformed? What can these snapshots over time tell me about their unending journey through life?

FRIENDSHIPS AND FITTING IN

Teresa

By the time Teresa reached the end of her elementary school career, she had developed a circle of friends. These consisted of children from her Integrated Play Groups and the fourth/fifth-grade classroom in which she was included. She spent a considerable amount of time with several girls who had formed a kind of clique. Together the girls hung out in the lunchroom, on the playground, in the school hallways, and in the girls' bathroom. Since many of the children were bused to school from different parts of the city, Teresa had few opportunities to visit her friends outside the school environment. She nevertheless maintained contact with some of her girlfriends from play groups by talking on the telephone.

In middle school, Teresa continued her friendships with the few girls from elementary school who happened to attend the same school. While enrolled in a special day class for children with learning disabilities and attending general education classes for a large portion of the day, Teresa established a new network of friends.

Once Teresa entered high school, she began referring to herself as a "young lady" and insisted that others acknowledge her status as a young lady as well. Although she remained immature and extremely naive in comparison with typical teenagers, many of her interests, concerns, and dreams for the future were strikingly similar to those of her peers. For instance, when questioned about her social life, Teresa eagerly recited a long list of girls with whom she "hung out" in school. When asked whether she was interested in any boys, she simply giggled and resisted further discussion on this topic. Among interests she had in common with other "young ladies" her age were the latest cosmetics, hairstyles, fashion, movies, television shows, and soap opera stars.

Like most teenagers, Teresa expressed her desire for independence. She volunteered in a day-care center and stated her interest in working with "little kids" in the future. Teresa also articulated her strong desire to be a mother in the future, perhaps influenced by the fact that she spent a great deal of time reading books to her younger brother and helping her mother care for him. When I questioned her about what she thought it would be like to be a mother, Teresa replied, "When I growing up to be a mother, I going to drive a car and move in my own apartment."

Freddy

In his last year at Loma Vista, Freddy also developed a small circle of friends from play groups and other integrated classroom experiences. His father noted that since being in play groups, Freddy had "come out of his shell" and made an effort to socialize with other children. In free play, I no longer had to prompt him to invite friends to join him or to enter an established game. He easily approached children with whom he was familiar and clearly articulated his desire to be with them.

Freddy's friends were equally devoted to him, making certain that he be included in all their activities and major events. Sook even described Freddy as her "best friend." Initiated and supported by Sook and his other friends, Freddy participated in the grand finale performance in the fifth-grade talent show. On graduation day, two friends accompanied him to the podium as he nervously delivered a speech that they had helped him prepare and rehearse.

The significance of Freddy's relationship with his friends came to the surface on the last day of school in a most unexpected and profound way. At the end of that day, I accompanied Freddy as he said his farewells to students with whom he had formed relationships in the fourth- and fifth-grade classes. Saying good-bye to his former play group friends, Carlos and Sook, proved to be a most moving and unforgettable experience.

> Freddy anxiously enters room 201, where students busily clean their desks to mark the end of another school year. Making his way through the chatter of friendly hellos, he approaches his two former playmates, Carlos and Sook, who happen to be standing side by side. Freddy states in a routinelike and stilted fashion, "Good-bye Carlos, good-bye Sook, I miss you, have a nice summer." Freddy then hugs Carlos and Sook as they each say good-bye and wish him well. As their embraces end, and Freddy turns to leave, tears begin to swell in Carlos's and Sook's eyes. Unaware, Freddy continues out the door, leaving Carlos and Sook behind, tears streaming down their crimson faces.

Freddy and Jared remained inseparable friends after leaving elementary school. Perhaps this was fate, since they attended the same middle school and high school programs. Although they particularly enjoyed certain activities together, they rarely had occasion to get together after school, because they lived far apart in the city. On several occasions during this time, Freddy telephoned to ask me to take him and Jared to Sausalito in my car, a trip we had taken together in the past.

Freddy developed other friendships in middle school that included students from his mainstreamed classes. In high school this proved to be more of a problem, since his special education program did not emphasize socialization with students from general education. Freddy nevertheless continued to express a desire to fit in and be accepted by his peer group. He maintained many of the same interests as those of his peer group, including sports and computer games. As is typical for youngsters approaching first adolescence and then adulthood, Freddy also wished to be recognized as older and mature and as having a distinct cultural identity. In middle school he replaced Freddy with Fred as his name of choice, and in high school he replaced Fred with his original Latino name, Federico.

Jared

Jared similarly developed social relationships with peers outside the play group environment. Although less reciprocal in nature than the friendships Teresa and Freddy experienced, they were nevertheless meaningful in the sense that Jared and his associates looked forward to spending time together and enjoyed one another's company. Jared had a particular following of about three boys from the fifth grade who took care to include him in all their activities and events. They did not baby him or tease him as he earlier experienced at times in play groups; rather they sought to get his attention through initiating activities they knew he enjoyed and accompanying him to significant events. Jared began to associate his friends with pleasurable experiences such as playing certain games, attending sports events, and going on various field trips. He often greeted his friends with smiles or an arm around the shoulder in anticipation of these mutually enjoyed activities.

Freddy continued to be Jared's number-one companion. Throughout middle school and high school, Jared had difficulty forming new relationships with peers on his own. His middle school teacher made an effort to foster opportunities for Jared to participate in activities with peers from the general education program, but as previously described, Jared had few opportunities for social integration with typical peers in high school.

Unlike Teresa and Freddy, who aspired to fit in with their peer group, Jared never overtly expressed this desire. He instead simply blended in most of the time without putting forth an effort. With his quiet and passive demeanor and fashionable eyeglasses, he often gave the impression of being a rather serious student. Since his family took great care of and pride in Jared's appearance, he always appeared immaculate in grooming and dress. Jared even ironed all his own clothes before school. Although placing so much emphasis on Jared's appearance may seem superficial in light of his social difficulties, this may have allowed him to be more like his peers, since adolescents often strive to blend in while struggling to find their identity.

FANTASY, GAMES, AND OTHER AMUSEMENTS

Teresa

Beyond the parameters of play groups, Teresa extended her joy in pretend play into related activities common to other girls her age. Within her circle of girlfriends at Loma Vista, she secretly rehearsed a performance for the annual fifth-grade talent show.

> On the day of the mystery performance, Teresa and her girlfriends busily prepare themselves in the girls' bathroom, dressing up in long, flowing, floral skirts, applying eye shadow and lipstick to their faces, and periodically twirling in front of the mirror. Nervous chatter, giggles, and occasional screams spread contagiously among the girls. Periodically, they poke their heads around the door,

teasing and chiding a group of boys. When it is finally their turn to perform, the girls nervously cling to each other, hurrying them- selves to the stage. As the curtains open, a popular song with a Caribbean beat plays—"La Bamba." For a moment, Teresa appears frozen as her girlfriends swing and sway their hips and arms. A second or two later, she follows suit, gracefully moving her body in rhythm to the music. Each girl dances in an entirely unique style, some more purposeful and perfected than others. Teresa seems to move spontaneously and without inhibition, as though the music flows from her very soul to her limbs.

When Teresa was 13, she was invited to spend a day playing with two girls she had not met before. Perhaps because of the unfamiliarity of the situation, she was exceedingly quiet and subdued. The manner in which she expressed herself in play, however, seemed to transcend shyness. As is typical of children in middle childhood, Teresa no longer overtly ex- pressed herself in make-believe play. Unlike in earlier play sessions, she ceased to give verbal play-by-play accounts of the sequence of events. She no longer relied on self-directed speech to guide her actions. Her behavior suggested that a subtle transformation had taken place in which she par- ticipated in private thought or fantasy to guide her play (Luria, 1982; Singer & Singer, 1990). In addition, the language she used was altogether socially directed for the purpose of establishing a shared reference to the play as well as to jointly plan and carry out an invented story line.

Teresa and her peers engage in conversation as they groom and dress the dolls.

TERESA: We have to go to the fair.
JULIE: OK . . . we can put the dress on her.
TERESA: Where we have to go to the fair, when we come right
    back? . . . Huh?
JENNY: Yeah, we can go on the rides.
TERESA: We going to roller coaster.
JULIE: Yeah, and then after the roller coaster, we can go on the
    merry-go-round.
TERESA: Mer . . . mer . . . merry go round.
JENNY: Then we can go to the Ferris wheel.
TERESA: Ferris wheel. There, we all dressed, huh, we all dressed,
    we all dressed. We dressing for fair.
JULIE: Now we can go get our coats on.
TERESA: We're going to the fair at 6:00. Put your coat on?

JULIE: Yeah, now we can go to the fair.
TERESA: (*Whispers to her baby doll.*) Yes.

Following this discussion, the girls acted out taking their dolls to the fair as they had planned. They took their dolls not only on the roller coaster, merry-go-round, and Ferris wheel but also on an entirely new ride, which Teresa invented and demonstrated with her doll.

Although Teresa gave up her dolls and pretend play as she entered high school at the age of 15, her earlier play interests continued to have a place in her adolescent years as appropriate and functional activity. She pursued her former fascination with hairstyles, makeup, jewelry, and fashion, comparing herself to teens her own age. She also continued to engage in earlier passions that revolved around household chores. She felt compelled to perfect her skills as a cook, cleaner, and caretaker, and her family expressed a great deal of pride in Teresa's effectiveness as a contributing household member. In particular, she learned to care for her baby brother, feeding, changing, and even scolding him when necessary. Once while talking on the telephone with me, Teresa excused herself to admonish him: "Now I told you to keep your feet off the furniture . . . you never listen." Apparently exasperated, Teresa commented to me, "Geesh! I told him to keep his feet down . . . he never listens."

Freddy

Freddy also extended his play interests to activities outside play groups. He transferred his budding capacity for pretend play into dramatic roles in school events and productions. On career day he enacted the role of a basketball player, demonstrating his moves for a group of students. He performed as a Wild Thing in the production of Maurice Sendak's (1983) *Where the Wild Things Are*, creating his own costume out of a paper sack, complete with glaring yellow eyes. He also participated in a Native American festival in which he helped to make costumes, props, scenery, and a feast and enacted songs and rituals with the other children.

Freddy easily incorporated his fascination with television, video, and cameras into hands-on experience as a member of the Loma Vista Video Club. With a group of students from different classrooms in the upper grades, he attended workshops to learn to operate the video equipment, videotaped special events, and even helped to put together a feature production.

Freddy's interests in games and sports began to take over as he grew older. Games with rules, such as the card game Uno were big favorites for many years. His earlier fixation on his little red ball developed into a passion for basketball. He spent most of his time shooting hoops, taking turns with Jared and other guys hanging out on the courts. He never quite made it into the "big leagues," but he nevertheless enjoyed playing as well as he could.

Freddy was able to transform his former obsession with groceries and other products into functional activity. Through community-based instruction in middle school and high school, he learned to shop and prepare food for meals. This was also reinforced at home, where he contributed to household chores. Freddy also assisted his uncle in his grocery store with various job-related tasks.

Jared

Jared extended his former preoccupation and interests into functional and appropriate activity. He participated in many of the same activities as Freddy, including putting on the production of his favorite book, *Where the Wild Things Are* (Sendak, 1983). While performing in the wild rumpus scene, he displayed more enthusiasm and animated expression than ever before. Jared was also a member of the Loma Vista Video Club and learned how to operate the equipment beside his peers. Like Freddy, he enjoyed playing the card game Uno with his small group of friends. He also joined Freddy and his other friends in shooting hoops on the basketball court.

Throughout middle school and high school, Jared continued to give great attention to the computer. He was especially appreciative of the opportunity to combine his two loves—the world of television games and the world of computers. He played the computer version of the Wheel of Fortune, from the game show of that name, with near perfection, quickly memorizing all the phrases after a few rounds. According to his family, he continued to watch a great deal of television at home, gravitating to his old favorite, *Jeopardy*, as well as to sports events—with the volume at ear-piercing level.

CREATIVE AND CONVENTIONAL EXPRESSIONS

Teresa

Teresa's passion for reading continued as she grew older. In middle school, she developed a particular fondness for reading fairy tales to her younger brother. Out of this she created her own stories and pictures, which clearly represented the "flowering of literary imagination" (Gardner, 1982).

Cinderella and the Seven Dwarfs

Once upon a time there was a Cinderella was staying with her stepmother and Cinderella was lost her one shoe, and the Snowwhite was feeding the kids some supper, and Snowwhite was setting the table, with the kids to eat at the table. Cinderella was Going up to her room to read her Book By her self. The Sleepy was eating her supper, and Cinderella is like to Dance with her stepsisters in the Dance party, and the Snowwhite was cried herself to sleep, with Cinderella was doing in Bed resting too. The Snowwhite was the mother, and sleepy, happy, sneezy, were outside playing the Ball, and Snowwhite said Get Over here! and Cinderella call Stepmother, comehere, and Stepmother said Go to your room Cinderella.

The end

Teresa's story appears to be typical of those by children entering kindergarten, who are able to "conjure up complex narratives involving a number of characters who carry out different sequences of behavior—sometimes consistent, sometimes inconsistent with one another, but always filled with spirit and life" (Gardner, 1982, p. 176). At first glance, Teresa's story does not seem to follow a logical sequence. Yet after questioning her and piecing together the different characters and events, one could logically decipher its meaning. Knowing that Snow White was both Cinderella's mother and stepmother, and that Sleepy, Happy, and Sneezy were the kids, made it possible to follow the story line. After writing this story, Teresa read it aloud, inserting drama and laughter and acknowledging its humor by saying, "It's a silly story, huh?"

Teresa's accompanying picture of Snow White and Cinderella standing beside their house and garden was similarly imaginative in nature. While this picture resembled many of her earlier drawings in its content, there were dramatic differences in overall style. In particular, this picture represented a cohesive and integrated piece of work. She incorporated more detail, bringing together the major elements of the picture.

On the day Teresa created this story and picture, she eagerly read aloud the original version of Lewis Carroll's (1867/1963) *Alice's Adventures in Wonderland*. In the first chapter, in which Alice falls down the rabbit hole, Teresa expressed concern while reading this passage: "Dinah'll miss me very much to-night, I should think! [Dinah was the cat.] I hope they'll remember her saucer of milk at tea-time. Dinah, my dear! I wish you were down here with me!" (p. 4). Teresa stated in a heart-filled voice, "She [Alice] scared and sad, she all alone 'cause she misses Dinah, she misses her cat."

Her description of Alice denoted not only her ability to understand the centrality of problems in stories, but also her capacity to empathize, to participate in the feelings of a fictional character.

In high school, Teresa wrote several letters to me that offered examples of her effort to integrate several events occurring at different points in time. The following excerpts highlight changes in her writing over a 3-year period.

Age 14 years:

I was taking two classes today, and I was taking English and P.E. then I Don't Have a chance to call you. Because the line was Busy. but you not home. and I was at School, and I try to call you Again, and I saw my Friend at the playground at the End of Summer.

Age 15 years:

I was walking through the track outside, and I was in Madrigal High school, and I Miss you to Pam then you will come to visit to My school next week. then I Miss you Again, you will go to Mexico, and I will be going to the 10th grade, then I going to be 16 years old.

Age 16 years:

I had a Terrific Summer this Year. I Went to Girl Scout camp on July 6. I Went swimming, my counselors were Tina, Evelyn and Diane. and all the campers went to the flag. we went to the Dining Hall. all my campers had Dinner there. I ate camp Food for Eight Days. We Sang Songs.

Freddy

As Freddy grew older, he gradually extended his repertoire of spoken and written language. Although he clearly made great efforts to articulate his interests and desires to others, he relied on his communicative partners to keep the conversation flowing. His one-sided approach to voicing his intentions was often difficult to override and redirect, as when he telephoned me on several occasions with the request to take him and his friend Jared on an outing.

PAMELA: Hello.
FREDDY: Pamela, when you coming?
PAMELA: Hello, is this Freddy?

FREDDY: No, Federico, when you coming?

PAMELA: Federico, how are you?

FREDDY: Fine, how are you? When you coming? I want to go to
Sausalito, ferry boat.

PAMELA: You want to go to Sausalito?

FREDDY: When you coming?

PAMELA: You want me to take you there?

FREDDY: Yes, when you coming, red Honda, pick up Jared,
Sausalito ferry boat.

PAMELA: But . . . I don't think I'll be able to take you and Jared to
Sausalito.

FREDDY: When you coming? Pick up Jared, red Honda, I want to go
to Sausalito, ferry boat. When you coming?

PAMELA: Why don't I make a visit to your school instead?

FREDDY: Pamela, when you coming? Pick up Jared, red Honda,
Sausalito, ferry boat.

Despite the circuitous pattern in which Freddy spoke, he demonstrated
his ability to hold in his mind visual images of a familiar event and to piece
these together into a logical sequence. He clearly knew what it was he
wished to do and managed to get his point across through spoken language.
The fact that this conversation took place on the telephone reinforced that
he could now express himself with words as opposed to relying on idiosyncratic gestures and expressions to impart meaning. Yet had this
conversation taken place in person, Freddy may have more easily com-
prehended my meaning with my own use of gesture and facial expression
to highlight my position.

Freddy similarly made advances in his written expression. While in
middle school, he wrote the following letter.

Age 13 years:

Dear Pamela,

How are you?

I am doing fine at my new school.

I miss you, Pamela

I like my new school.

I play baseball on the computer.

I also go to PE and played basketball.

From,

Fred

Hernandez

In high school, he sent a holiday greeting card with a brief letter enclosed. In this letter, he was able to piece together different bits of pertinent information that as a whole was easy to comprehend and also added a meaningful flavor of sentiment.

Age 16 years:

Happy Holidays
Hi Pamela—Im glad to hear From you I still Think of You! I am doing good aT school Hope You are Fine was wishing you a Happy Holiday We are Have vacation as you know

Jared

Although Jared's spoken and written language remained severely impaired, he continued to make slow but steady progress over the years. His repertoire of spontaneous spoken language expanded, consisting of a number of stored echolalic phrases and simple sentences. These he retrieved when making requests or comments associated with familiar routines or events. In social situations, Jared continued to be highly imitative, echoing speech and behavior patterns when unable to comprehend his communicative partner. With prompting and redirection, Jared could carry on a somewhat predictable, although meaningful, conversation.

PAMELA: Hello, Jared, how are you?
JARED: Fine thanks.
PAMELA: Do you know who this is?
JARED: Who this is.
PAMELA: This is Pamela, your teacher from Loma Vista.
JARED: Pamela, Pamela, Pamela.
PAMELA: Do you remember Loma Vista?
JARED: Yes.
PAMELA: Who were your friends at Loma Vista? Do you remember your friends in play groups?
JARED: Play groups, yes.
PAMELA: Do you remember Carlos . . . and . . .
JARED: Carlos, Noah, Ronny.
PAMELA: How is school?
JARED: School, fine thanks.
PAMELA: What is your favorite thing in school? Do you like computers?
JARED: Computers, yes.
PAMELA: What do you like to do on the computer?

JARED: Computers, yes. I want computer. I want Wheel of Fortune.
PAMELA: Do you like to play Wheel of Fortune on the computer?
JARED: Yes, I want to play Wheel of Fortune.
PAMELA: Oh, I miss you, Jared.
JARED: I miss you, Pamela.

Jared's joy in reading continued over the years, but his pleasure largely derived from decoding the written word rather than from interpreting its meaning. Thus his capacity to spontaneously express himself through written language had limits similar to the limits on his spoken language. He nevertheless continued to write more expressively with the aid of an adult or more capable peer. For instance, he recently sent a photo of himself in a holiday greeting card with endearments contrived with the help of his family members.

Merry X mas
Happy New Year's
I miss you and your smile
I Love you very much!
I Love and mess you
Jared age 16

INTERPRETIVE SUMMARY

Teresa, Freddy, and Jared's journey into play continued for as long as they were permitted to hold on to their childhood. In elementary school, they had each established a network of friends. They showed that they could coordinate a variety of social activities with peers outside the Integrated Play Groups context. Moreover, they fully participated in functional activities, events, and creative performances commonly enjoyed by children of a similar age. Once Teresa, Freddy, and Jared entered middle and secondary school, occasions for establishing and maintaining peer relationships and participating in imaginative activities diverged from earlier experiences. They faced ever-increasing challenges to comprehend and adapt to the volatile nature of adolescence and the demands of school. In one way or another, they each found ways to establish friendships and conform to the patterns of activity prevalent in their peer culture. They each held on to many of their earlier interests, pursuing them in different ways through fantasy, games, and other amusements. They similarly conveyed meaning to others in different ways through creative and conventional expressions.

C H A P T E R   1 2

Conclusion: Implications for Theory and Practice

There are few things more fascinating or informative than learning about the experience of other conscious beings as they make their way through the world. Accounts of their lives have a power to move us deeply, to help us imagine what it must have been like to live in different social and historical circumstances, to provide insights into the workings of lives, and perhaps to provide a frame of reference for reassessing our own experience, own fortunes, own possibilities of existence.

—William M. Runyan, *Life Histories and Psychobiography: Explorations in Theory and Method*

IN THE PRECEDING chapters, I attempted to accurately portray Teresa, Freddy, and Jared's personal struggles and triumphs as they made their way into the play culture of their peers (see Table 12.1 for an overview of Teresa, Freddy, and Jared's passage to play culture). Ethnography offered a means to capture in depth and detail the evolution of each child's social and symbolic development embedded within everyday life and patterns of sociocultural activity, focusing on Integrated Play Groups. By sharing their stories, I hope to enhance our understanding of both theory and practice in order to make a meaningful difference in the lives of children with autism.

The questions and methods guiding my interpretations called for exploration from various theoretical viewpoints. I wondered about the extent to which children with autism are capable of socially coordinated and imaginative play; the qualitative processes underlying emerging capacities for reciprocal social relations and symbolic representation in play,

Table 12.1. Overview of Teresa, Freddy, and Jared's Passage to Play Culture

SOCIAL RELATIONS WITH PEERS

	5 to 9 years		9 to 11 years in Integrated Play Groups		11 to 16 years	
	UNCHARTED TERRITORY	BEGINNING TO EXPLORE	ENTERING PLAY	GUIDED PARTICIPATION	EMBRACING PLAY	AN UNENDING JOURNEY
	Alone in Company of Children	*Noticing Other Children*	*Subtle Attempts to Participate*	*Socially Coordinated Play*	*Acceptance and Membership*	*Friendships and Fitting In*
Teresa	Little or no social contact with peers	Watches peers; Some parallel play	Idiosyncratic approaches; Brief exchanges	Joint focus; Joint action; Role enactment	Role enactment; Role-playing	Friendships; Supported peer relations
Freddy	Little or no social contact with peers	Watches peers; Some parallel play; Joint action—Jared	Idiosyncratic approaches; Brief exchanges	Joint focus; Joint action; Role enactment	Joint action; Role enactment/ some role-playing	Friendships; Supported peer relations
Jared	Little or no social contact with peers	Watches peers; Some parallel play; Joint action—Freddy	Idiosyncratic approaches; Brief exchanges	Joint focus; Joint action	Joint focus/action; Some role enactment	Supported peer relations

TRANSFORMATIONS IN PLAY

	UNCHARTED TERRITORY	BEGINNING TO EXPLORE	ENTERING PLAY	GUIDED PARTICIPATION	EMBRACING PLAY	AN UNENDING JOURNEY
	Creating Order Through Rituals	*Ritualizing Familiar Routines*	*Gravitating to Rules and Rituals*	*Symbolic Representation*	*Budding Flowers of Pretend*	*Fantasy, Games, Amusements*
Teresa	Stereotyped manipulation and functional play	Stereotyped functional play	Stereotyped manipulation and functional play	Conventional functional play; Simple/advanced pretend	Simple pretend; Advanced pretend	Advanced pretend; Fantasy play
Freddy	Stereotyped sensorimotor and manipulation play	Stereotyped manipulation and functional play	Stereotyped manipulation and functional play	Conventional functional play; Simple/some advanced pretend	Conventional functional play; Simple/some advanced pretend	Conventional games and sports
Jared	Stereotyped sensorimotor play	Stereotyped sensorimotor play	Stereotyped sensorimotor play	Conventional manipulation and functional play	Conventional functional play; Some simple pretend	Conventional games and sports

TRANSFORMATIONS IN WORDS AND PICTURES

	Imitating Sounds and Signs	Discovering Meaning in Words and Pictures	Conveying Meaning in Words and Pictures	Creative and Conventional Expressions
Teresa	Nonfocused echolalia—single words Reads/writes name and alphabet	Focused echolalia—word combinations and stored phrases Emerging literacy From simple to realistic representation in drawing	Self- and other-directed complex speech Storylike scripts in language, play and writing Symbolic/creative representation in drawing	Socially directed complex speech Literary imagination Empathy for characters in complex stories Rich and elaborate detail in drawing
Freddy	Nonfocused echolalia—single words Reads products and advertisements	Focused echolalia—word combinations Increased reading vocabulary Begins to write Simple designs and representation in drawing	Focused echolalia—stored phrases Spontaneous comments Reads/writes simple sentences and stories Realistic and some symbolic representation in drawing	Gradually extends repertoire Spontaneous verbal and written language
Jared	Nonfocused echolalia—single words Reads simple words in familiar books	Focused echolalia—word combinations Hyperlexia Repetitive writing Simple designs and representation in drawing	Focused echolalia—word combinations Hyperlexia Writes memorized text Realistic and some symbolic representation in drawing	Gradually extends repertoire echolalic speech—word combinations and stored phrases

spoken language, writing, and drawing; and the systems of social support that mediate social and symbolic growth.

I found sociocultural and social constructivist theories particularly amenable for interpreting the complex processes involved in social and symbolic development. Rather than viewing development as an independent, cumulative, and linear process, I recognized the children's emerging social and symbolic capacities as major transformations of mind, mediated through social participation in culturally defined activity. According to Vygotsky (1978):

> Child development is a complex dialectical process characterized by periodicity, unevenness in the development of different functions, metamorphosis or qualitative transformation of one form into another, intertwining of external and internal factors, and adaptive processes which overcome impediments that the child encounters. (p. 73)

SOCIAL CONSTRUCTION OF IMAGINATION

An examination of changes over time suggests that in the context of supported peer play, Teresa, Freddy, and Jared displayed growing capacities for reciprocal social interaction and symbolic representation in unique ways. This general observation corresponds to foundational studies in which children with autism showed increases in social interaction and produced more sophisticated and diverse forms of play (functional, symbolic, or both) when supported by an adult in contexts of peer play activity (Lord, 1984; McHale, 1983; Wolfberg & Schuler, 1993). A further discovery was that Teresa, Freddy, and Jared each showed some capacity to socially coordinate actions and thoughts with peers before evidence of more conventional play and imagination emerged.

Socially Coordinated Play

Socially coordinated play required that each play partner (novice and expert) establish reciprocal, two-way interactions such that there was a mutual exchange of activity or language even when one partner took on more of a supportive role to maintain the interaction (Bretherton, 1984; Garvey, 1977; Howes et al., 1992). Socially coordinated play varied from child to child.

Jared learned to participate in simple turn-taking using objects (building a block tower) or social games (hide-and-seek) as vehicles for *joint action*. Beyond joint action, Freddy learned *role enactment*, portraying real-life activities through conventional actions in social pretend play scripts (pushing a shopping cart, loading it with groceries, and handing items to a cashier). Beyond role enactment, Teresa learned *role-playing*, taking on pretend roles with dolls and other people as well as using objects in imaginary ways within complex and elaborate social pretend play scripts (taking reciprocal roles of mother and baby with a doll, pretending to take the baby to the bathroom while going shopping with peers).

Teresa, Freddy, and Jared appeared to follow a similar progression in establishing varying degrees of social coordination in play. They each began to show an interest in other children and their activities by watching them, using their materials, and imitating their actions. They each were able to establish a common focus with peers on a particular activity in play groups, but only with support from a more experienced player or adult. Once this occurred, Teresa, Freddy, and Jared each progressed in a different manner to achieve what appeared to be her or his full potential for socially coordinated play.

In Teresa's case, she seemed to progress rapidly from joint action to role enactment, and then suddenly burst into role-playing. Freddy seemed to move gradually from joint action to role enactment, and on occasion he touched on role-playing when a peer created the context for him, scaffolding within his zone of proximal development. Jared seemed to remain at a stage of joint action, although he, too, occasionally touched on role enactment when a peer created the context through structured support.

The capacities to establish joint action, role enactment, and role-playing, respectively, appeared in natural sequence corresponding to an increased sense of social awareness and shared understanding. Based on the accumulated evidence, one might speculate that social reciprocity propelled symbolic advances in play, spoken language, writing, and drawing. This is consistent with Bruner's (1982) and Vygotsky's (1978) proposition that adults and more capable peers may be helpful in structuring and scaffolding higher levels of performance.

> An essential feature of learning is that it creates the zone of proximal development; that is, learning awakens a variety of internal developmental processes that are able to operate only when the child is interacting with people in his environment and in cooperation with his peers. (Vygotsky, 1978, p. 90)

Symbolic Representation in Play

In all cases, the children spontaneously generated more diverse and complex forms of play than previously exhibited in independent play activity. These play forms were manifested differently for each child, corresponding to relative advances in socially coordinated play. These also appeared to follow a natural sequence along the symbolic dimension of play, ranging from *functional play* directed to concrete objects; to *simple pretend* directed to oneself, dolls, and other agents; to *advanced pretend* involving symbolic transformations with objects, role-taking with dolls and other agents, and integrating complex scripts (Harris, 1989; Leslie, 1987; Ungerer & Sigman, 1981). Here I have chosen to make a distinction between functional play with a focus on directing acts to objects and simple pretend play with a focus on directing acts to self, others, and dolls using realistic props.

In joint action, Jared learned to play in a functional manner using constructive toys and realistic replicas, only occasionally directing isolated simple pretend play acts to himself, dolls, and others. These generally reflected immediate or delayed imitation of a peer's actions (saying, "Hello," on the telephone; patting the baby doll; and saying, "Baby"). It is difficult to determine whether Jared connected any of his play acts with familiar events outside play groups. One might presume that he was familiar with the use of a telephone in other social contexts. Nevertheless, he appeared to be highly dependent upon physical objects and actions within the play group context in order to generate anything novel in his play repertoire. He was clearly locked into a literal mode, not yet able to understand the meaning of his new play combinations.

In joint action and role enactment, Freddy also learned to play in a functional manner with constructive toys and realistic props, but in more flexible ways than Jared. He integrated several simple pretend play schemes directed to himself, dolls, and other agents. Freddy also showed the capacity for more advanced forms of pretend by transforming objects in play (molding Play-Doh into the shape of a burrito, calling it a burrito, pretending to eat it, and saying, "Mmmm, delicious"). Although Freddy's inspiration certainly derived from watching his peers in play, he did not always literally imitate his peers the way Jared did. Freddy's play acts evidently had social meaning for him, since they had association with his life experience outside the play group context. Moreover, these play acts were indicative of Freddy's budding imagination, representing a transition from a literal to nonliteral mode.

Teresa's budding imagination fully blossomed as she made a transition from role enactment to role-playing in social pretend play. She first imitated her peers' actions, gestures, and vocalizations ("echoplaylia") before launching into her own unique variations on play themes. This was a turning point at which she proceeded to advanced pretend play, producing symbolic transformations, including object substitution, attribution of absent or false properties, and invention of imaginary objects. She enacted various roles with dolls and other children, and even engaged in reciprocal role taking. She planned and integrated multiple events within coherent and evolving play scripts. Teresa connected her life experiences to her play, which included adopting and creating social roles of significant adults. Her play themes generally corresponded to familiar social events in her life until she was older, at which point she interjected fantasy.

Symbolic Representation in Words and Pictures

Changes in the symbolic dimension of play seemed to appear in tandem with changes in verbal expression, written expression, and representations in drawings, although not in precisely the same manner. Parallel advances in language and symbolic play, in particular, suggested a common representational core (McCune-Nicholich & Bruskin, 1982). These changes similarly reflected a growing awareness and connection to the social world. Although Jared did not show significant advances in his spoken language from the time he began play groups, he more consistently produced echolalic utterances that served a greater variety of communicative functions, including commenting to share a social event with his peers and teacher. He appeared to be highly dependent upon people and their actions within the play group context to prompt verbal utterances. Jared's writing was similarly highly imitative, but also more diversified in that he no longer repeated the same word without variation. Instead, he spontaneously reproduced written information the way Teresa had when she first began to write. Similarly, his drawings grew to be somewhat more realistic and connected to his life experiences. In effect, he attempted to portray what he saw in the physical world experienced with others.

Although Teresa progressed to a more sophisticated level than that of Freddy, they followed a somewhat similar pattern in developing spoken language, writing, and drawing. They each had linguistic repertoires consisting of immediate and delayed echolalic utterances associated with familiar people, routines, and television commercials. They each later showed more spontaneous and complex forms of language than was evident prior to the guided-participation phase in play groups. As they did in their play, they began to break down repetitive patterns and generate novel words, phrases, and sentences. Freddy showed greater competence in language when guided by an adult. Teresa's language production was consistent in exchanges with both adults and peers. Similarly, they each showed more complex forms of language in their written expression. Freddy benefited from adult guidance in constructing sentences and short stories connected to his social experiences.

In Teresa's case, a more flexible and cohesive narrative structure spontaneously emerged in both her play and her writing. While collaborating on play scripts with peers, she organized and integrated sequences into play scripts of her own. She reconstructed familiar events in recitations resembling narratives heard in the bedtime monologues of young children (Bruner, 1990; Weir, 1976). Through these monologues Teresa "played" with language, reordering events into meaningful and coherent stories. As Nelson and Seidman (1984) proposed, the "art of conversation" and make-believe may be well served by established play scripts and peer interaction.

Collateral changes also appeared in Teresa's and Freddy's representations in drawing and painting. They similarly broke down repetitive patterns in pictures to represent people, objects, and events. Their drawings grew to be more conventional in nature, depicting realistic themes related to a variety of life experiences. Freddy's pictures seemed to show his physical and social world as connected but not integrated. Teresa's pictures, on the other hand, showed that she integrated her physical and social world into coherent themes and stories.

If the coordination of social action and thought fueled further cognitive and linguistic growth, one might view these advances as the crystallization of social experience. In Teresa's case, she eventually learned to construct a shared understanding of literal and nonliteral meaning with her peers in social pretend play, suggesting an increased capacity to understand the social perspectives of others. The fact that Teresa learned to initiate and enter into peer interactions in a more effective manner, took on roles as well as reciprocated roles in sociodramatic play with dolls and other children, ascribed emotions and intentions to dolls, depicted social transactions between characters in her writing and drawing, and expressed empathy for characters while reading stories provided evidence for at least a rudimentary form of appreciating the existence of mental states in others.

OTHER POSSIBLE INFLUENCES

What else do Teresa, Freddy, and Jared's stories tell us? Certainly, each child's unique experience had as much to do with who they were as individuals as it did with the play culture of which they became a part. Although play culture reflects the social worlds children construct together separate from adults, they do not exist in a vacuum—they are clearly embedded within the larger sociocultural contexts of family, school, and community. The transactional influences within these circles of culture are virtually limitless. Nevertheless, one might speculate about the nature of these transactions and their influences on Teresa, Freddy, and Jared's patterns of development and social experience.

Emotional Security and Attachments

Examination of advances over time suggests considering issues of emotional security and attachments to primary and secondary caregivers (family members, teachers) as connected to advances in Teresa, Freddy, and Jared's play. As posited in the attachment literature (Ainsworth, 1982), young children will more readily explore their surroundings and engage in playful behavior when securely attached to one or more major caregivers. The sense of predictability and security afforded by consistent caregiving and unconditional acceptance was likely an impetus for Teresa, Freddy, and Jared to venture out and explore the rather elusive world of play. This possibly enabled them to be less insistent on routines and breakdown patterns of ritualistic behavior that once served to provide structure of and control over their environment. Moreover, Teresa was able to transfer her sense of comfort and well-being from caring adults to a personal object of affection (her doll Morrell), signifying a point of entry into pretend play. In a less conventional manner, Freddy and Jared seemed to regard each other as "objects" of affection, which possibly afforded a certain sense of comfort before they explored new dimensions in play.

Social Interpreters and Guides

Social mediation, involving guidance from me, my colleagues, and more experienced players as support partners appeared to be instrumental in establishing a context for social coordination on all levels to occur. In Integrated Play Groups and related peer cultural contexts, my colleagues and I took on the role of social interpreter and guide. To arrange opportunities for natural participation in joint activity necessitated creating an atmosphere of mutual respect in which every child was seen as a competent and contributing member of the group. The capacity to interpret children's initiations in play, particularly when subtle or unconventional in nature, may have been critical to establishing a common ground on which the children related to one another. In addition, the ability to provide the children with just the right amount and type of support—ranging from directing activities and interaction to pulling back and observing—seemed to facilitate the process of social collaboration and play on various levels.

The extent to which we adults feel at ease with violation of norms and lack of predictability may determine our effectiveness in scaffolding play skills. After all, play in its purest form invites continual redefinition of norms, since there are no predetermined rules or goals. Thus, the ability to relinquish control, allowing children to take the lead and set the tone in establishing reciprocal and imaginative play, may be an important aspect of being a social interpreter and guide. This may be particularly relevant to special educators, behavioral therapists, and related practitioners who are trained to take a directive role in delivering instruction to children who present problems in behavior and development. A compelling question is whether this capacity to yield control and adapt to changing patterns in children's play is a skill adults can learn or whether it is at least partially dependent on disposition. Based on our training efforts, we suspect it requires a combination of both (O'Connor, 1999; Wolfberg & Schuler, 1992). Some of our trainees seem to be, for one reason or another, unable to take other than a directive stance with children in play situations. In such cases, the structure of the relationship between the adult and child is hierarchical in nature, leaving little room for children to explore. For this reason, peer interactions may offer advantages over interactions with adults. As Rogoff (1990) pointed out, "It may be the absence of external control, the freedom to play with the rules themselves and to recast the goals of an activity from moment to moment, that is unique and valuable in peer interaction" (p. 117).

The value of peer interaction in the context of play is particularly relevant in delimiting the roles of the play guide and peers. As adults, we clearly cannot take the place of peers in play. Only children are the true experts when it comes to playing and creating a "play world." We can provide the structure and the impetus for this to happen, but we can never fully become a member of children's play culture. Nevertheless, to support children impaired in their ability to play naturally, we must to some degree enhance the expertise of "expert" players by acting as an interpreter and model.

Peer Responsiveness and Social Style

The responsiveness and unique social styles of expert players in Integrated Play Groups may have afforded Teresa, Freddy, and Jared different degrees of structure and predictability within a common play framework. Peer responsiveness to the different ways novice players communicated naturally influenced their capacity to participate in social activities and reciprocate as a playmate, partner, or friend.

While the expert players in Integrated Play Groups gradually adopted certain aspects of the adult guide role, rarely did they aspire to be adultlike figures. They very much retained their identities as "kids" playing and having fun, but with an added sense of responsibility to cooperate and include all members of the group. From the expert players' perspectives, this meant that they would have to make an effort to help the less-skilled players learn how to play by adapting to their different interests and styles of communication. Misha described her role as an expert player this way:

> I help the children to make decisions on their own about what they'd like to play with. After they make their decisions, I play with them. Sometimes I have to help them take turns and share. When I first started play groups, I had a few problems playing with the children. I felt funny, and I was afraid of some of the children. . . . I stopped feeling funny and started to like them. We learned to play a special hide-n-go-seek, and we learned to have patience with the children.

Carlos's perception of his role as an expert player revealed that the process of learning how to communicate and play together got easier as the play group participants got to know each other. Ultimately, this resulted in having fun and becoming "good friends."

> When I first started [play groups], it felt funny. It was really hard at first to play with all of the children. They ran away and did their own things. Later on it felt a little easier because they knew us better. Then . . . we learned ways to communicate and play to-gether. Th[at] was fun. A month later we were all good friends. I learned how to get along with all of them. I liked it very much because I never knew them before. I also learned to communicate with all the children.

While expert players learned new skills to recognize and respond to novice players' idiosyncratic initiations in play, these skills did not account for their personal styles in fostering different types of interactions in play. Keila often took dominant roles (such as mother figure) in social pretend play that gave her unprecedented authority to tell the others what to do. This seemed to add more structure and predictability to play scenarios. Carlos and Noah similarly took on authoritarian pretend roles (store man-ager, police officer), but they often clowned around while giving orders. This seemed to add flexibility to structured play events. Sook, Misha, Dina, and Ronny, on the other hand, were more like "doting aunts and uncles" who affectionately watched over the novice players to make sure they stayed involved and on top of things, sometimes teasing them in a playful fashion. This, too, appeared to provide structure, but in a manner that more resembled scaffolding. All these types of interactions apparently afforded opportunities for the children to weave together their different play inter-ests within a common framework of either constructive or social pretend play. These types of interactions and their influences on social interaction and play would be interesting to explore in the future.

Novice Experience and Competence in Play

The extent to which Teresa, Freddy, and Jared relied on me, my colleagues, or expert players to support them in play varied with respect to their experience and competence in play. This is consistent with Lord and Magill's (1989) proposition that the degree to which children with autism are socially responsive to others in play is dependent upon the quality and severity of the child's social impairment, experience, and familiarity with particular peers and play events, as well as the structure of play activities.

In Integrated Play Groups, all three children produced more sophisticated play with my guidance, but only Teresa transferred her newly acquired skills to play with experienced peers without my being present. She learned to rely on her peers rather than me to respond to her initiations. It is possible that expert players more consistently responded to Teresa's initiations because she had developed more conventional means with which to communicate and initiate play. This enabled Teresa to successfully gain entry into peer groups and coordinate social pretend play activities with and without me or other adults being present.

Freddy and Jared, on the other hand, transferred some of what they had learned with me to their play with experienced peers, but they exhibited more socially coordinated, diverse, and complex forms of play when I was present. They seemed to rely more on me for cues and support to expand their play. Moreover, since Freddy and Jared continued to initiate play in obscure ways, it is possible that their peers also relied more on me for interpretation than in Teresa's case. Freddy and Jared nevertheless succeeded in entering and coordinating social play activities without my being present on occasions when peers responded to their cues. When not collaborating on play scripts in some form or fashion, the children had opportunities to observe and play in parallel to peers. This in itself may have added to their experience, as they later imitated and practiced what they had observed within a collaborative framework.

Redefining Norms in Play Culture

The desire or drive to be accepted by one's peer group and to belong to a larger culture of children's play was possibly of greatest relevance to the observed changes. Yet without me or another adult to interpret, nurture, and guide participation in play, Teresa, Freddy, and Jared would likely have remained outsiders on the fringes of their peer play culture. The Integrated Play Groups model, as described here, possibly allows for greater acceptance and understanding of differences than other interventions that heavily emphasize conformity to patterns of conventional activity and social structures. Play, in itself, provides room for exploration and discovery within a larger zone of proximal development, since norms, standards, and expectations are only marginally defined.

In Integrated Play Groups, inclusion in children's play culture seemed to hinge on the formation of a group identity that went beyond simple tolerance to full appreciation and unconditional acceptance of peer differences. The construction of a peer-group identity that continually redefined and shaped the meaning of "normal" enabled Teresa, Freddy, and Jared to safely emulate peers, try on new social hats, and form friendships within an ever-widening social network. Perhaps play is the ultimate context for social inclusion, since it sanctions variation and allows for multiple perspectives.

NEW AND FUTURE DIRECTIONS

Given the nature of ethnography, we are left with many more questions than answers through the telling of Teresa, Freddy, and Jared's stories. The original questions, themes, and hypotheses that emerged from this study continue to be relevant to our ongoing research and practice.

A general observation indicated that supported peer play aroused and nurtured each child's capacity for reciprocal social interaction and symbolic representation in qualitatively different ways. Based on our collective research findings to date, we surmise that large-scale replications of the IPG model will continue to yield similar patterns in overall sociability and imagination (Wolfberg et al., in preparation). More extensive research will also allow us to address questions concerning the interdependence of socially mediated support, children's play culture, and various domains of social and symbolic growth. Further clarification of these interrelationships will enhance our theoretical understanding of autism and the design of effective and meaningful interventions.

Teresa, Freddy, and Jared's stories lend support to the supposition that a combination of social and performance factors potentially explain problems in symbolic operations commonly ascribed to autism (Harris, 1993; Jarrold et al., 1993; Jordan, 2003). It is possible that these three children developed within the symbolic dimension of play at different rates in a relatively consistent sequence corresponding to normal patterns of development. If children with autism are indeed delayed in play, then one might speculate that manifestations of their spontaneous play resemble those of their developmental counterparts, surfacing in unusual ways because of the difficulties associated with a "different kind of mind"—mindblindness, weak central coherence, executive dysfunction, and experiences of the embodied or enactive mind. With social mediation, each child generated more conventional play forms. Only Teresa developed the full capacity for pretend play, but she never actually reached the level of sophistication of her peers. It would be important to ascertain whether the experiences of Teresa, Freddy, and Jared speak to those of other children with autism, represent rare and unusual cases, or correspond to subgroups within the spectrum of autism.

Teresa, Freddy, and Jared's stories also have implications for the role of guided peer play experiences in supporting social inclusion at school and in the community (Hanson et al., 1998; Wolfberg, 2008; Wolfberg et al., 2008; Wolfberg, LePage, & Cook, in press). Related to this, we are interested in the extent to which IPGs contribute to long-term peer relationships (particularly friendships) and the nature of these relationships. Through our research, we hope to address the issue of preparing typically developing children for the influx of their peers with autism in society today (Wolfberg et al., in preparation). With 1 in 150 children receiving a diagnosis of autism, there is a growing need to demystify autism and its symptoms so that typical peers may come to understand and delight in the company of children with autism. We plan to further explore the influence of IPGs on typical children and examine not only changes in their understanding of autism after participation in the IPGs, but also changes in their judgments about fairness and the inclusion and exclusion of children with autism in activities with typical peers.

Recognizing the unlimited potential of play is especially critical for the design of education and therapy programs concerned with quality and effectiveness (Banks et al., 2005; Dunn Buron & Wolfberg, 2008; Iovannone et al., 2003; Wolfberg & Schuler, 2006). In order for all children to reap the benefits of play, education and therapy need alternative models commensurate with the "spirit of play." Now more than ever, the field needs to embrace holistic models of instruction and intervention that reflect this spirit.

"Community of learners" is one such model that supports students through guided discovery in a holistic and meaningful curriculum (Brown & Campione, 1990; Rogoff, Matusov, & White, 1998). Implicitly valuing diversity of ability, cultural background, and learning styles, this model affords children multiple opportunities to share expertise and find their own niche in collaboration with peers.

Programs that build on Howard Gardner's (1983, 1999) theory of multiple intelligences encapsulate a vision in which play and imagination are an integral part of the curriculum. Children discover, explore, and develop those domains where they have natural curiosity and talent while participating in a rich array of hands-on activities in special interest groups featuring apprenticeships in a variety of topics.

In the innovative "play school" of Reggio Emilia, Italy, children are immersed in creative and meaningful projects that involve a collective effort. There is a dual focus on individual and group exploration, discovery, and invention in an atmosphere of joy. According to the former education director Loris Malaguzzi:

> Creativity is a kind of continuously evolving fantasy, and you don't know when a child will grab at that fantasy. What we like to do is to accompany a child as far as possible into the realm of the creative spirit. But we can do no more. At the end of the path is creativity. We don't know if the children will want to follow the path all the way to the end, but it is important that we have shown them not only the road, but also that we have offered them the instruments—the thoughts, the words, the rapport, the solidarity, the love—that sustain the hope of arriving at a moment of joy. (cited in Goleman, Kaufman, & Ray, 1992, p. 83)

Such models of play and imagination—that exploit children's natural proclivities to explore, create, and construct meaning in collective activity—extend an invitation to diversity and inclusion.

References

Ainsworth, M. (1982). Attachment: Retrospect and prospect. In C. M. Park & J. Stevenson-Hinde (Eds.), *The place of attachment in human behavior* (pp. 3–30). New York: Basic Books.

American Psychiatric Association. (1994). *Diagnostic and statistical manual of mental disorders-IV*. Washington, DC: Author.

American Psychiatric Association. (2000). *Diagnostic and statistical manual of mental disorders-IV-TR*. Washington, DC: Author.

Asperger, H. (1944). Die autistischen Psychopathen im Kindersalter. *Archiv für Psychiatrie und Nervenkrankheiten, 117*, 76–136.

Attwood, A., Frith, U., & Hermelin, B. (1988). The understanding and use of interpersonal gestures by autistic and Down syndrome children. *Journal of Autism and Developmental Disorders, 18*, 241–257.

Axline, V. (1947). *Play therapy*. New York: Ballantine Books.

Banks, J., Cochran-Smith, M., Moll, L., Richert, A., Zeichner, K., LePage, P., Darling-Hammond, L., & Duffy, H. (2005). Teaching diverse learners. In L. Darling-Hammond & J. Bransford (Eds.), *Preparing teachers for a changing world: What teachers should learn and be able to do* (pp. 232–274). San Francisco: Jossey-Bass.

Baron-Cohen, S. (1987). Autism and symbolic play. *British Journal of Developmental Psychology, 5*(2), 139–148.

Baron-Cohen, S. (1988). Social and pragmatic deficits in autism: Cognitive or affective? *Journal of Autism and Developmental Disorders, 18*, 379–402.

Baron-Cohen, S. (1995). *Mindblindness: An essay on autism and theory of mind*. Boston: MIT Press.

Baron-Cohen, S., Leslie, A. M., & Frith, U. (1985). Does the autistic child have a theory of mind? *Cognition, 21*, 37–46.

Bauminger, N., & Kasari, C. (2000). Loneliness and friendship in high-functioning children with autism. *Child Development, 71*(2), 447–456.

Beckman, P. J., & Kohl, F. L. (1984). The effects of social and isolate toys on the interactions and play of integrated and nonintegrated groups of preschoolers. *Education and Training of the Mentally Retarded, 19*, 169–175.

Bednersh, F., & Peck, C. A. (1986). Assessing social environments: Effects of peer characteristic on the social behavior of children with severe handicaps. *Child Study Journal, 16*(4), 315–329.

Bemporad, J. R. (1979). Adult recollections of a formerly autistic child. *Journal of Autism and Developmental Disorders, 9,* 179–197.

Berk, L., Mann, T., & Ogan, A. (2006). Make-believe play: Wellspring for development and self-regulation (pp. 74–100). In D. G. Singer, R. Golinkoff, & K. Hirsh-Pasek (Eds.), *Play = learning: How play motivates and enhances children's cognitive and social-emotional growth.* New York: Oxford University Press.

Bernard-Optiz, V., Ing, S., & Kong, T. K. (2004). Comparison of behavioral and natural play interventions for children with autism. *Autism: International Journal of Research and Practice, 8*(3), 319–333.

Bettelheim, B. (1967). *The empty fortress: Infantile autism and the birth of the self.* New York: Free Press.

Boucher, J., & Lewis, V. (1990). Guessing or creating? A reply to Baron-Cohen. *British Journal of Developmental Psychology, 8,* 205–206.

Boucher, J., & Wolfberg, P. J. (Eds.). (2003). Editorial [Special issue on play]. *Autism: The International Journal of Research and Practice, 7*(4), 339–346

Bretherton, I. (Ed.). (1984). *Symbolic play: The development of social understanding.* Orlando, FL: Academic Press.

Brown, A. L., & Campione, J. C. (1990). Communities of learning and thinking, or A context by any other name. *Human Development, 21,* 108–125.

Bruner, J. S. (1982). The organization of action, and the nature of adult-infant transaction. In E. F. Tronick (Ed.), *Social interchange in infancy: Affect, cognition, and communication* (pp. 25–35). Baltimore: University Park Press.

Bruner, J. S. (1990). *Acts of meaning.* Cambridge, MA: Harvard University Press.

Bruner, J. S., & Sherwood, V. (1976). Peek-a-boo and the learning of role structures. In J. S. Bruner, A. Jolly, & K. Sylva (Eds.), *Play: Its role in development and evolution* (pp. 277–285). New York: Penguin.

Carroll, L. (1963). *Alice's adventures in wonderland and through the looking glass.* New York: Macmillan. (Original work published 1867)

Carter, A., Davis, N. O., Klin, A., & Volkmar, F. (2005). Social development in autism (pp. 312–334). In F. Volkmar, R. Paul, A. Klin, & D. Cohen (Eds.), *Handbook of autism and pervasive developmental disorders* (3rd ed.). Hoboken, NJ: Wiley & Sons.

Casner, M. W., & Marks, S. F. (1984, April). *Playing with autistic children.* Paper presented at the annual convention of the Council for Exceptional Children, Washington, DC.

Cazden, C. B. (1976). Play with language and metalinguistic awareness: One dimension of language experience. In J. S. Bruner, A. Jolly, & K. Sylva (Eds.), *Play: Its role in development and evolution* (pp. 603–608). New York: Basic Books.

Centers for Disease Control and Prevention. (2008). *Autism Information Center.* Retrieved June 29, 2008, from http://www.cdc.gov/ncbddd/autism/

Chamberlain, B., Kasari, C., & Rotheram-Fuller, E. (2007). Involvement or isolation? The social networks of children with autism in regular classrooms. *Journal of Autism and Developmental Disorders, 37,* 230–242.

Charman, T., & Baron-Cohen, S. (1997). Brief report: Prompted pretend play in autism. *Journal of Autism and Developmental Disorders, 27*(3), 325–332.

Chudacoff, H. (2007). *Children at play: An American history.* New York: New York University Press.

Cohen, D., & MacKeith, S. A. (1991). *The development of imagination: The private worlds of childhood.* London: Routledge.

Coles, R. (1992). *Their eyes meeting the world: The drawings and paintings of children.* Boston: Houghton Mifflin.

Corsaro, W. (2005). *Sociology of childhood* (2nd ed.). Thousand Oaks, CA: Pine Forge Press.

Dawson, G., & Adams, A. (1984). Imitation and social responsiveness in autistic children. *Journal of Abnormal Child Psychology, 12,* 209–225.

Denzin, N. (1978). Sociological methods: Critical reflections and the logic of naturalistic inquiry. In N. Denzin (Eds.), *Sociological methods: A source book* (pp. 1–29). New York: McGraw-Hill.

Dewey, D., Lord, C., & Magil, J. (1988). Qualitative assessment of the effect of play materials in dyadic peer interactions of children with autism. *Canadian Journal of Psychology, 42*(2), 240–260.

Dewey, J. (1902). *The child and the curriculum.* Chicago: University of Chicago Press.

DiSalvo, C., & Oswald, D. (2002). Peer-mediated socialization interventions for children with autism: A consideration of peer expectancies. *Focus on Autism and Other Developmental Disabilities, 17,* 198–207.

Dissanayake, C., Sigman, M., & Kasari, C. (1996). Long-term stability of individual differences in the emotional responsiveness of children with autism. *Journal of Child Psychology and Psychiatry, 37*(4), 462–467.

Dodge, K. A., Schlundt, D. C., Schocken, I., & Delugach, J. D. (1983). Social competence and children's sociometric status: The role of peer group entry strategies. *Merrill-Palmer Quarterly, 29,* 309–336.

Dominguez, A., Ziviani, J., & Rodger, S. (2006). Play behaviours and play object preferences of young children with autistic disorder in a clinical play environment. *Autism, 10*(1), 53–69.

Donnelly, J., & Bovee, J-P. (2003). Reflections on play: Recollections from a mother and son with AS. *Autism: International Journal of Research and Practice, 7*(4), 471–476.

Dunn, J. (2004). *Children's friendships: The beginnings of intimacy.* Oxford: Blackwell.

Dunn, W. (2008). Sensory processing: Identifying patterns and support strategies. In K. Dunn Buron & P. J. Wolfberg (Eds.), *Learners on the autism spectrum: Preparing highly qualified educators* (pp. 138–159). Shawnee Mission, KS: Autism Asperger.

Dunn Buron, K., & Wolfberg, P. J. (Eds.). (2008). *Learners on the autism spectrum: Preparing highly qualified educators.* Shawnee Mission, KS: Autism Asperger.

Dyson, A. H. (1991). The roots of literacy development: Play, pictures, and peers. In B. Scales, M. Almy, A. Nicolopoulou, & S. Ervin-Tripp (Eds.), *Play and the social context of development and early care and education* (pp. 98–116). New York: Teachers College Press.

Eisen, G. (1988). *Children and play in the Holocaust: Games among the shadows.* Amherst: University of Massachusetts Press.

Elkind, D. (1981). *The hurried child, growing up too fast*. Boston: Addison-Wesley.

Elkind, D. (2007). *The power of play: How spontaneous, imaginative activities lead to happier, healthier children*. Cambridge, MA: Da Capo Press.

Ellis, M. J. (1973). *Why people play*. Englewood Cliffs, NJ: Prentice-Hall.

Erikson, E. H. (1950). *Childhood and society*. New York: Norton.

Ervin-Tripp, S. (1991). Play in language development. In B. Scales, M. Almy, A. Nicolopoulou, & S. Ervin-Tripp (Eds.), *Play and the social context of development in early care and education* (pp. 84–97). New York: Teachers College Press.

Fenson, L., & Schell, R. E. (1986). The origins of exploratory play. In P. K. Smith (Eds.), *Children's play: Research developments and practical applications* (pp. 15–38). New York: Gordon & Breach Science.

Ferrara, C., & Hill, S. (1980). The responsiveness of autistic children to the predictability of social and nonsocial toys. *Journal of Autism and Developmental Disorders, 10*, 51–57.

Filipek, P. A. (2005). Medical aspects of autism. In F. R. Volkmar, R. Paul, A. Klin, & D. Cohen (Eds.), *Handbook of autism and pervasive developmental disorders* (3rd ed., pp. 534–578). New York: Wiley.

Fombonne, E. (2005). Epidemiological studies of pervasive developmental disorders. In F. R. Volkmar, R. Paul, A. Klin, & D. Cohen (Eds.), *Handbook of autism and pervasive developmental disorders* (3rd ed., pp. 42–69). New York: Wiley.

Freud, A. (1946). *The psychoanalytic treatment of children*. London: Imago. (Original work published 1926)

Freud, S. (1961). *Beyond the pleasure principle*. New York: Norton. (Original work published 1920)

Frith, U. (2003). *Autism: Explaining the enigma* (2nd rev. ed.). Oxford, UK: Blackwell.

Frith, U., & Happe, F. (1994). Autism: Beyond "theory of mind." *Cognition, 50*, 115–132.

Fromberg, D., & Bergen, D. (2006). *Play from birth to twelve and beyond: Contexts, perspectives, and meaning* (2nd ed.). London: Routledge.

Gardner, H. (1982). *Art, mind, and brain: A cognitive approach to creativity*. New York: Basic Books.

Gardner, H. (1983). *Frames of mind: The theory of multiple intelligences*. New York: Basic Books.

Gardner, H. (1989). *To open minds*. New York: Basic Books.

Gardner, H. (1999). *Intelligence reframed*. New York: Basic Books.

Gardner, H., Wolf, D., & Smith, A. (1982). Max and Molly: Individual differences in early artistic symbolization. In H. Gardner (Eds.), *Art, mind, and brain: A cognitive approach to creativity* (pp. 110–127). New York: Basic Books.

Garvey, C. (1977). *Play*. Cambridge, MA: Harvard University Press.

Glaser, B. G., & Strauss, S. L. (1967). *The discovery of grounded theory: Strategies for qualitative research*. Chicago: Aldine Press.

Goldstein, H., & Cisar, C. L. (1992). Promoting interaction during sociodramatic play: Teaching scripts to typical preschoolers and classmates with disabilities. *Journal of Applied Behavior Analysis, 25*, 265–280.

Goleman, D., Kaufman, P., & Ray, M. (1992). *The creative spirit*. New York: Dutton.

Gonsier-Gerdin, J. (1992). *Elementary school children's perspectives on peers with dis-*

abilities in the context of Integrated Play Groups: "They're not really disabled. They're like plain kids." Unpublished position paper, University of California at Berkeley with San Francisco State University.

Greenspan, S. I., & Wieder, S. (1997). An integrated developmental approach to interventions for young children with severe difficulties in relating and communicating. *Zero to Three, 17,* 5–18.

Groos, K. (1901). *The play of man.* New York: Appleton.

Hall, G. S. (1906). *Youth.* New York: Appleton.

Hanson, M. J., Wolfberg, P. J., Zercher, C., Morgan, M., Gutierrez, S., Beckman, P., & Barnwell, D. (1998). The culture of inclusion: Recognizing diversity on multiple levels. *Early Childhood Research Quarterly, 13*(1), 185–209.

Haring, T. G., & Lovinger, L. (1989). Promoting social interaction through teaching generalized play initiation responses to preschool children with autism. *Journal of the Association for Persons with Severe Handicaps, 14*(1), 58–67.

Harris, P. (1993). Pretending and planning. In S. Baron-Cohen, H. Tager-Flusberg, & D. J. Cohen (Eds.), *Understanding other minds: Perspectives from autism* (pp. 228–246). New York: Oxford University Press.

Harris, P. L. (1989). *Children and emotion: The development of psychological understanding.* Oxford, UK: Blackwell.

Hartup, W. W. (1983). Peer relations. In M. Heatherington (Eds.), *Handbook of child psychology* (pp. 103–196). New York: John Wiley & Sons.

Hauge, D. (1988). *Using child initiated object manipulations to develop social, communicative responsiveness in children with autism and severe disabilities.* Unpublished master's thesis, San Francisco State University.

Hay, D. F., Payne, A., & Chadwick, A. (2004). Peer relations in childhood. *Journal of Child Psychology and Psychiatry, 45,* 84–108.

Heath, S. B. (1989). The learner as cultural member. In M. L. Rice & R. L. Schiefelbusch (Eds.), *The teachability of language* (pp. 330–350). Baltimore: Paul H. Brookes.

Heinrichs, R. (2003). *Perfect targets: Asperger syndrome and bullying—practical solutions for surviving the social world.* Shawnee Mission, KS: Autism Asperger.

Hermelin, B. (2001). *Bright splinters of the mind: A personal story of research with an autistic savant.* London: Jessica Kingsley.

Hill, E. L. (2004). Executive dysfunction in autism. *Trends in cognitive science, 8,* 1, 26–31.

Hill, E. L., & Frith, U. (2003). Understanding autism: Insights from mind and brain. *Philosophical Transactions of the Royal Society Series B, 358,* 281–289.

Hobson, R. P. (2005). What puts the jointness into joint attention? In N. Eilan, C. Hoerl, T. McCormack, & J. Roessler (Eds.), *Joint attention: communication and other minds: Issues in philosophy and psychology* (pp. 185–204). New York: Oxford University Press.

Howes, C., Unger, O., & Matheson, C. C. (1992). *The collaborative construction of pretend.* Albany: State University of New York Press.

Howlin, P. (1986). An overview of social behavior in autism. In E. Schopler & G. B. Mesibov (Eds.), *Social behavior in autism* (pp. 103–132). New York: Plenum.

Hughes, C. (2001). *Executive dysfunction in autism: Its nature and implications for everyday practice*. In J. A. Burack, T. Charman, N. Yirimiya, and P. R. Zelazo (Eds.), *The development of autism: Perspectives from theory and research* (pp. 255–275). Mahwah, NJ: Erlbaum.

Ingersoll, B., & Schreibman, L. (2002). *The effect of reciprocal imitation training on imitative and spontaneous pretend play in children with autism*. Paper presented at the 2nd International Meeting for Research on Autism, Orlando, FL.

Iovannone, R., Dunlop, G., Huber, H., & Kincaid, D. (2003). Effective educational practices for students with ASD. *Focus on Autism and Other Developmental Disabilities, 18*(3), 150–165.

Isaacs, S. (1933). *Social development in young children*. London: Routledge & Kegan Paul.

Isenberg, J., & Quisenberry, N. (2002). *Play: Essential for all children*. Position paper of the Association for Childhood Education International. Retrieved September 28, 2008, from www.acei.org/playpaper.htm

Jarrold, C. (2003). A review of research into pretend play in autism. *Autism: The International Journal of Research and Practice, 7*(4), 379–390.

Jarrold, C., Boucher, J., & Smith, P. (1993). Symbolic play in autism: A review. *Journal of Autism and Developmental Disorders, 23*(2), 281–307.

Jarrold, C., Boucher, J., & Smith, P. (1996). Generativity deficits in pretend play in autism. *British Journal of Developmental Psychology, 14*, 275–300.

Jordan, R. (2003). Social play and autistic spectrum disorders. *Autism: The International Journal of Research and Practice, 7*(4), 347–360.

Kafai, Y. (2006). Play and technology: Revised realities and potential perspectives (pp. 207–214). In D. Fromberg & D. Bergen (Eds.), *Play from birth to twelve and beyond: Contexts, perspectives, and meaning* (2nd ed.). London: Routledge.

Kalmanson, B., & Pekarsky, J. H. (1987). Infant parent psychotherapy with an autistic toddler. *Infant Mental Health Journal, 8*(4), 330–355.

Kanner, L. (1943). Autistic disturbances of affective contact. *Nervous Child, 2*, 217–250.

Klein, M. (1955). The psychoanalytic play technique. *American Journal of Orthopsychiatry, 25*, 223–237.

Klin, A., Jones, W., Schultz, R., & Volkmar, F. (2003). The enactive mind, or from actions to cognition: Lessons from autism. *Philosophical Transactions of the Royal Society: Biological Sciences, 358*, (1430), 345–360.

Koegel, L. K., Koegel, R. L., Harrower, J. K., & Carter, C. M. (1999). Pivotal response intervention: Overview of approach. *Journal of the Association for Persons with Severe Handicaps, 24*, 174–185.

Kok, A. J., Kong, T. Y., & Bernard-Opitz, V. (2002). A comparison of the effects of structured play and facilitated play approaches on preschoolers with autism: A case study. *Autism: International Journal of Research and Practice, 6*, 181–196.

Kupfersmidt, J. B., & Dodge, K. A. (Eds.). (2004). *Children's peer relations: From development to intervention*. Washington, DC: American Psychological Association.

Ladd, G. W. (2005). *Children's peer relations and social competence: A century of progress*. New Haven, CT: Yale University Press.

Lakoff, G., & Johnson, M. (1999). *Philosophy in the flesh: The embodied mind and its challenge to Western thought.* New York: Basic Books.

Lane, H. (1979). *The wild boy of Aveyron.* Cambridge, MA: Harvard University Press.

Lantz, J. F., Nelson, J. M., & Loftin, R. L. (2004). Guiding children with autism in play: Applying the Integrated Play Group Model in school settings. *Exceptional Children, 37*(2), 8–14.

Lave, J., & Wenger, E. (1991). *Situated learning: Legitimate peripheral participation.* Cambridge, UK: Cambridge University Press.

Leaf, R., & McEachin, J. (1999). *A Work in Progress: Behavior Management Strategies and a Curriculum for Intensive Behavioral Treatment of Autism.* New York: DRL.

Leslie, A. M. (1987). Pretense and representation: The origins of "theory of mind." *Psychological Review, 94,* 412–426.

Levine, M. (2002). *A mind at a time.* New York: Simon & Schuster.

Lewis, V., & Boucher, J. (1988). Spontaneous, instructed and elicited play in relatively able autistic children. *British Journal of Developmental Psychology, 6*(4), 325–339.

Libby, S., Powell, S., Messer, D., & Jordan, R. (1998). Spontaneous play in children with autism: A reappraisal. *Journal of Autism and Developmental Disorders, 28*(487), 97.

Lifter, K., Sulzer-Azaroff, B., Anderson, S., & Cowdery, G. (1993). Teaching play activities to preschool children with sisabilities: The importance of developmental considerations, *Journal of Early Intervention, 17*: 139–159.

Lord, C. (1984). Development of peer relations in children with autism. In F. Morrison, C. Lord, & D. Keating (Eds.), *Applied developmental psychology* (pp. 165–229). New York: Academic Press.

Lord, C., & Hopkins, M. J. (1986). The social behavior of autistic children with younger and same-age nonhandicapped peers. *Journal of Autism and Developmental Disorders, 16*(3), 249–262.

Lord, C., & Magill, J. (1989). Methodological and theoretical issues in studying peer-directed behavior and autism. In G. Dawson (Eds.), *Autism: New directions in diagnosis and treatment* (pp. 326–345). New York: Guilford Press.

Lovaas, O. I. (1987). Behavioral treatment and normal educational and intellectual functioning in young autistic children. *Journal of Consulting and Clinical Psychology, 55,* 3–9.

Luria, A. R. (1982). *Language and cognition.* New York: Wiley & Sons.

Mahler, M. (1952). On child psychosis in schizophrenia: Autistic and symbiotic infantile psychosis. In R. S. Eissler, A. Freud, H. Hartmann, & K. Kris (Eds.), *Psychoanalytic study of the child* (pp. 265–305). New York: International University Press.

Maurice, C., Green, G., & Luce, S. C. (1996). *Behavioral intervention for young children with autism: A manual for parents and professionals.* Austin, TX: Pro-Ed.

McCracken, H. (2005). Friend 2 Friend: Fostering mutual friendships for children with ASD. *Autism-Asperger Digest, 1,* 6–15.

McCune-Nicholich, L. (1981). Toward symbolic functioning: Structure of early pretend games and potential parallels with language. *Child Development, 3,* 785–797.

McCune-Nicholich, L., & Bruskin, C. (1982). Combinatorial competency in symbolic play and language. In D. J. Pepler & K. H. Rubin (Eds.), *The play of children: Current theory and research* (pp. 30–45). Basel, Switzerland: Karger.

McHale, S. (1983). Social interactions of autistic and nonhandicapped children during free play. *American Journal of Orthopsychiatry, 53*(1), 81–91.

Meyer, L. H., Fox, A., Schermer, A., Ketelsen, D., Montan, N., Maley, K., & Cole, D. (1987). The effects of teacher intrusion on social play interactions between children with autism and their nonhandicapped peers. *Journal of Autism and Developmental Disorders, 17*(3), 315–332.

Mikaelan, B. (2003). *Increasing language through sibling and peer support play.* Unpublished master's thesis, San Francisco State University.

Minshew, N., & Williams, D. (2008). Brain-behavior connections in autism (pp. 44–65). In K. Dunn & P. Wolfberg (Eds.), *Learners on the autism spectrum: Preparing highly qualified educators.* Shawnee Mission, KS: Autism Asperger.

Mirenda, P. (2003). Toward functional augmentative and alternative communication for students with autism: Manual signs, graphic symbols, and voice output communication aids. *Language, Speech, and Hearing Services in Schools, 34*, 202–215.

Mittledorf, W., Hendricks, S., & Landreth, G. L. (2001). Play therapy with autistic children. In G. L. Landreth (Ed.), *Innovations in play therapy.* New York: Routledge.

Mouritsen, F. (1996). *Play culture: Essays on child culture, play, and narratives.* Odense, Denmark: Odense University.

Müller, E., Schuler, A. L., & Yates, G. (2008). Social challenges and supports from the perspective of individuals with Asperger syndrome and other autism spectrum disabilities. *Autism: International Journal of Research and Practice, 12*(2), 173–190.

Mundy, P., Sigman, M. D., Ungerer, J., & Sherman, T. (1986). Defining the social deficits of autism: The contribution of non-verbal communication measures. *Journal of Child Psychology and Psychiatry and Allied Disciplines, 27*(5), 657–669.

National Research Council. (2001). *Educating children with autism. Committee on educational interventions for children with autism.* Washington, DC: National Academy Press.

Nelson, K., & Seidman, S. (1984). Playing with scripts. In I. Bretherton (Eds.), *Symbolic play: The development of social understanding* (pp. 299–336). Orlando, FL: Academic Press.

Nicholich, L. (1977). Beyond sensorimotor intelligence: Assessment of symbolic maturity through analysis of pretend play. *Merrill-Palmer Quarterly, 23*(2), 89–99.

Nicolopoulou, A., McDowell, J., & Brockmeyer, C. (2006). Narrative play and emergent literacy: Storytelling and story-acting meet journal writing (pp. 124–144). In D. G. Singer, R. Golinkoff, & K. Hirsh-Pasek (Eds.), *Play = learning: How play motivates and enhances children's cognitive and social-emotional growth.* New York: Oxford University Press.

Nuzzolo-Gomez, R., Leonard, M. A., Ortiz, E., Rivera, C. M., & Greer, R. D. (2002).

Teaching children with autism to prefer books or toys over stereotypy or passivity. *Journal of Positive Behavior Interventions, 4*, 60–67.

O'Connor, T. (1999). *Teacher perspectives of facilitated play in Integrated Play Groups.* Unpublished master's thesis, San Francisco State University.

Odom, S., & Strain, P. (1984). Peer-mediated approaches to promoting children's social interaction: A review. *American Journal of Orthopsychiatry, 54*(4), 544–557.

Odom, S., & Strain, P. (1986). Comparison of peer-initiation and teacher antecedent interventions for promoting reciprocal social interaction of autistic preschoolers. *Journal of Applied Behavior Analysis, 19*, 59–71.

Oke, N. J., & Schreibman, L. (1990). Training social initiations to a high-functioning autistic child: Assessment of collateral behavior change and generalization in a case study. *Journal of Autism and Developmental Disorders, 20*, 479–497.

Page, L. G., & Smith, H. (1985). *The Foxfire book of toys and games: Reminisences and instructions from Appalachia.* New York: E. P. Dutton.

Paley, V. G. (1990). *The boy who would be a helicopter: The uses of storytelling in the classroom.* Cambridge, MA: Harvard University Press.

Park, C. C. (1967). *The siege: The first eight years of an autistic child.* Boston: Little, Brown.

Parten, M. B. (1932). Social participation among preschool children. *Journal of Abnormal and Social Psychology, 27*, 243–269.

Patton, M. Q. (2002). *Qualitative research and evaluations methods* (3rd ed.). Newbury Park, CA: Sage.

Peck, C. A., Schuler, A. L., Tomlinson, C., Theimer, R. K., & Haring, T. (1984). *The social competence curriculum project: A guide to instructional communicative interactions.* Special Education Research Institute, University of California at Santa Barbara.

Pellegrini, A. (1985). Relations between symbolic play and literate behavior. In L. Galda & A. Pellegrini (Eds.), *Play, language, and story: The development of children's literate behavior* (pp. 79–97). Norwood, NJ: Ablex.

Pelligrini, A., & Smith, P. K. (2005). *The nature of play: Great apes and humans.* New York: Guilford Press.

Phyfe-Perkins, E. (1980). Children's behavior in preschool settings: A review of research concerning the influence of the physical environment. In L. G. Katz (Eds.), *Current topics in early childhhood education* (pp. 91–125). Norwood, NJ: Ablex.

Piaget, J. (1962). *Play, dreams, and imitation in childhood.* New York: Norton.

Pierce, K., & Schreibman, L. (1997). Using peer trainers to promote social behavior in autism: Are they effective at enhancing multiple social modalities? *Focus on Autism and Other Developmental Disabilities, 12*, 207–218.

Powell, M. (2007). The hidden curriculum of recess. *Children, Youth and Environments, 17*(4), 86–106.

Prizant, B., Wetherby, A., Rubin, E., Rydell, P., & Laurent, A. (2003). The SCERTS Model: A family-centered, transactional approach to enhancing communication and socioemotional abilities of young children with ASD. *Infants and Young Children, 16*(4), 296–316.

Putallaz, M. (1983). Predicting children's sociometric status from their behavior. *Child Development, 54*, 1417–1426.

Putallaz, M., & Gottman, J. M. (1981). An interactional model of children's entry into peer groups. *Child Development, 52*, 986–994.

Ragland, E. V., Kerr, M. M., & Strain, P. S. (1978). Effects of peer social initiations on the behavior of withdrawn autistic children. *Behavior Modification, 2*, 565–578.

Richard, V., & Goupil, G. (2005). Application des groupes de jeux integres aupres d'eleves ayant un trouble envahissant du development (Implementation of Integrated Play Groups with PDD students). *Revue quebecoise de psychologie, 26*(3), 79–103.

Richler, J., Bishop, S. L., Kleinke, R. R., & Lord, C. (2007). Restricted and repetitive behaviors in young children with autism spectrum disorders. *Journal of Autism and Developmental Disorders, 37*(1), 73–85.

Riddle, M. A. (1987). Individual and parental psychotherapy in autism. In D. Cohen & A. Donnellan (Eds.), *Handbook of autism and pervasive developmental disorders* (pp. 528–541). New York: Wiley & Sons.

Riguet, C., Taylor, N., Benaroya, S., & Klein, L. (1981). Symbolic play in autistic, Downs, and normal children of equivalent mental age. *Journal of Autism and Developmental Disorders, 11*(4), 439–448.

Rimland, B. (1964). *Infantile autism*. New York: Appleton-Century-Crofts.

Roeyers, H. (1996). The influence of nonhandicapped peers on the social interactions of children with a pervasive developmental disorder. *Journal of Autism and Developmental Disorders, 11*, 61–70.

Rogers, S. J., Hall, T., Osaki, D., Reaven, J., & Herbison J. (2000). The Denver model: A comprehensive, integrated educational approach to young children with autism and their families. In J. S. Handleman & S. L. Harris (Eds.), *Preschool education programs for children with autism* (2nd ed., pp. 95–133). Austin, TX: Pro-Ed.

Rogers, S., & Williams, J. (Eds.). (2006). *Imitation and the social mind: Autism and typical development*. New York: Guilford Press.

Rogoff, B. (1990). *Apprenticeship in thinking*. New York: Oxford University Press.

Rogoff, B., Matusov, E., & White, C. (1998). Models of teaching and learning: Participation in a community of learners. In D. Olson & N. Torrance (Eds.), *The handbook of education and human development*, New York: Wiley and sons.

Ross, H. S., & Kay, D. A. (1980). The origins of social games. In K. H. Rubin (Eds.), *Children's play* (pp. 17–31). San Francisco: Jossey-Bass.

Rousseau, J.-J. (1762/1956). *The "Emile" of Jean Jacques Rousseau: Selections*. New York: Teachers College Press. (Original work published 1762)

Rubin, K. H., Fein, G. G., & Vandenberg, B. (1983). Play. In E. M. Hetherington (Eds.), *Handbook of child psychology: Socialization, personality, and social development* (pp. 694–759). New York: John Wiley & Sons.

Rubin, K. H., & Thompson, A. (2003). *The friendship factor: Helping our children navigate their social worlds—and why it matters for their success and happiness*. New York: Penguin Books.

Runyan, W. M. (1982). *Life histories and psychobiography: Explorations in theory and method*. New York: Oxford University Press.

Rutter, M. (1978). Diagnosis and definition. In M. Rutter & E. Schopler (Eds.), *Autism: A reappraisal of concepts and treatment* (pp. 1–25). New York: Plenum Press.

Rutter, M. (2005). Genetic influences and autism. In F. R. Volkmar, R. Paul, A. Klin, & D. Cohen (Eds.), *Handbook of autism and pervasive developmental disorders* (3rd ed., pp. 425–452). New York: Wiley.

Sacks, O. (1995). *An anthropologist on Mars: Seven paradoxical tales*. New York: Knopf.

Santarcarangelo, S., Dyer, K., & Luce, S .C. (1987). Generalized reduction of disruptive behavior in unsupervised settings through specific toy training. *Journal of the Association for Persons with Severe Handicaps, 12*, 38–44.

Schaefer, C., & Kaduson, H. G. (Eds.). (2007). *Contemporary play therapy: Theory, research, and practice*. New York: Guilford Press.

Schuler, A. L. (2003). Beyond Echoplaylia: Promoting language in children with autism. In J. Boucher & P. Wolfberg (Eds.), *Autism: the International Journal of Research and Practice, 7*(4), 455–469.

Schuler, A., & Fletcher, C. (2002). Making communication meaningful: Cracking the language interaction code (pp. 41–52). In R. Gabriels & D. Hill (Eds.), *Autism: From research to individualized practice*. London: Jessica Kingsley.

Schuler, A. L., & Wolfberg, P. J. (2000). Promoting peer socialization and play: The art of scaffolding. In A. Wetherby & B. Prizant (Eds.), *Autism spectrum disorders: A transactional developmental perspective* (pp. 251–279). Baltimore: Paul H. Brookes.

Schwartzman, H. (1978). *Transformations*. New York: Plenum.

Selfe, L. (1977). *Nadia*. New York: Academic Press.

Selmer-Olsen, I. (1993). Children's culture and adult presentation of this culture. *International Play Journal, 1*, 191–202.

Sendak, M. (1983). *Where the wild things are*. New York: Scholastic.

Sherrat, D. (2002). Developing pretend play in children with autism: A case study. *Autism: International Journal of Research and Practice, 6*(2), 169–179.

Shores, R. E., Hester, P., & Strain, P. S. (1976). The effects of amount and type of teacher-child interaction on child-child interaction during free-play. *Psychology in the Schools, 13*, 171–175.

Sigman, M., & Ruskin, E. (1999). Continuity and change in the social competence of children with autism, Down syndrome, and developmental delays. *Monographs of the Society for Research in Child Development, 64*, 1–114.

Sigman, M., Spence, S. J., & Wang, A. T. (2006). Autism from developmental and neuropsychological perspectives. *Annual Review of Clinical Psychology, 2*, 327–355.

Sigman, M., & Ungerer, J. A. (1984). Cognitive and language skills in autistic, mentally retarded, and normal children. *Developmental Psychology, 20*, 293–302.

Singer, D. G., Golinkoff, R., & Hirsh-Pasek, K. (Eds.) (2006). *Play = learning: How play motivates and enhances children's cognitive and social-emotional growth*. New York: Oxford University Press.

Singer, D. G., & Singer, J. L. (1990). *The house of make-believe*. Cambridge, MA: Harvard University Press.

Singer, D. G., & Singer, J. L. (2006). Fantasy and imagination. In D. Fromberg & D. Bergen (Eds.), *Play from birth to twelve and beyond: Contexts, perspectives, and meaning* (2nd ed., pp. 370–378). London: Routledge.

Smilansky, S. (1968). *The effects of sociodramatic play on disadvantaged preschool children.* New York: Wiley

Smith, M. J. (2001). *Teaching play skills to children with autistic spectrum disorder: A practical guide.* New York: DRL.

Smith, P. K. (1963). *Games and songs of American children.* New York: Dover.

Smith, P. K., & Connolly, K. J. (1980). *The ecology of preschool behavior.* Cambridge, MA: Cambridge University Press.

Smith, P. K., Takhvar, M., Gore, N., & Vollstedt, R. (1986). Play in young children: Problems of definition, categorization, and measurement. In P. K. Smith (Eds.), *Children's play: Research developments and practical applications* (pp. 37–55). New York: Gordon & Breach Science.

Smith, P. K., & Vollstedt, R. (1985). On defining play: An empirical study of the relationship between play and various play criteria. *Child Development, 56,* 1042–1050.

Sorce, J. F., & Emde, R. N. (1981). Mother's presence is not enough: The effect of emotional availability on infant exploration. *Developmental psychology, 17,* 737–741.

South, M., Ozonoff, S., & McMahon, W. M. (2005). Repetitive behavior profiles in Asperger syndrome and high-functioning autism. *Journal of Autism and Developmental Disorders, 35*(2) 145–158.

Stahmer, A. C. (1995). Teaching symbolic play to children with autism using pivotal response training. *Journal of Autism and Developmental Disorders, 25,* 123–141.

Stahmer, A. C., Ingersoll, B., & Carter, C. (2003). Behavioral approaches to promoting play. *Autism: International Journal of Research and Practice, 7*(4), 401–413.

Staub, D. (1999). *Delicate threads: Friendships between children with and without special needs in inclusive settings.* Bethesda, MD: Woodbine House.

Stern, D. (1974). The goal and structure of mother-infant play. *Journal of the American Academy of Child Psychiatry, 13,* 402–421.

Stone, J. C., & Gonsier-Gerdin, J. (1995). *Educational evaluation: The interpretive paradigm.* Course reader, Educational Evaluation 273A. Graduate School of Education, University of California, Berkeley.

Strain, P. S. (1984). Social interactions of handicapped preschoolers in developmentally integrated and segregated settings: A study of generalization effects. In T. Field, J. L. Roopnarine, & M. Segal (Eds.), *Friendships in normal and handicapped children* (pp. 187–207). Norwood, NJ: Ablex.

Strain, P. S., Kerr, M. M., & Ragland, E. V. (1979). Effects of peer mediated social initiations and prompting/reinforcement on the social behavior of autistic children. *Journal of Child Psychology and Psychiatry, 18,* 167–178.

Strain, P., & Kohler, F. (1998). Peer-mediated social interventions for young children with autism. *Seminars in Speech and Language, 19,* 391–405.

Sutton-Smith, B. (1967). The role of play in cognitive development. *Young Children, 22,* 361–370.

Sutton-Smith, B. (2001). *The ambiguity of play.* Cambridge, MA: Harvard University Press.

Sylva, K., Bruner, J. S., & Genova, P. (1976). The role of play in the problem-solving of children 3–5 years old. In J. S. Bruner, A. Jolly, & K. Sylva (Eds.), *Play: Its role in development and evolution* (pp. 244–257). New York: Basic Books.

Tager-Flusberg, H., Paul, R., & Lord, C. (2005). Language and communication in autism. In F. Volkmar, R. Paul, A. Klin, & D. Cohen (Eds.), *Handbook of autism and pervasive developmental disorders* (3rd ed., pp. 335–364). New York: Wiley & Sons.

Taylor, M., Carlson, S. M., Maring, B., Gerow, L. E., & Charlie, C. (2004). The characteristics and correlates of high fantasy in school-aged children: Imaginary companions, impersonation, and social understanding. *Developmental Psychology, 40,* 1173–1187.

Thorp, D. M., Stahmer, A. C., & Schreibman, L. (1995). Teaching sociodramatic play to children with autism using pivotal response training. *Journal of Autism and Developmental Disorders, 25,* 265–282.

Tiegerman, E., & Primavera, L. (1981). Object manipulation: An interactional strategy with autistic children. *Journal of Autism and Developmental Disorders, 11*(4), 427–438.

Tilton, J. R., & Ottinger, D. R. (1964). Comparison of toy play behavior of autistic, retarded, and normal children. *Psychological Reports, 15,* 967–975.

Treffert, M. D. (2006). *Extraordinary people: Understanding savant syndrome.* New York: Ballantine Books.

Twachtman-Cullen, D. (2008). Symbolic communication: Common pathways and points of departure (pp. 88–113). In K. Dunn & P. Wolfberg (Eds.), *Learners on the autism spectrum: Preparing highly qualified educators.* Shawnee Mission, KS: Autism Asperger.

Ungerer, J. A., & Sigman, M. (1981). Symbolic play and language comprehension in autistic children. *Journal of the American Academy of Child Psychiatry, 20,* 318–337.

United Nations. (1959). Declaration of the rights of the child, Principle 7. General Assembly resolution 1386 (XIV), 14 U.N. GAOR Supp. (No. 16) at 19, U.N. Doc. A.4354.

Van Berckelaer-Onnes, I. A. (2003). Promoting early play. *Autism: International Journal of Research and Practice, 7*(4), 415–423.

Vygotsky, L. (1966). Play and its role in the mental development of the child. *Soviet Psychology, 12,* 6–18. (Original work published 1933)

Vygotsky, L. S. (1978). *Mind in society: The development of higher psychological processes.* Cambridge, MA: Harvard University Press.

Watson, J. S. (1976). Smiling, cooing, and "the game." In J. S. Bruner, A. Jolly, & K. Sylva (Eds.), *Play: Its role in development and evolution* (pp. 268–276). New York: Basic Books.

Weir, R. (1976). Playing with language. In J. S. Bruner, A. Jolly, & K. Sylva (Eds.), *Play: Its role in development and evolution* (pp. 609–618). New York: Basic Books.

Wellman, H. M. (1993). Early understanding of mind: The normal case. In S. Baron-Cohen, H. Tager-Flusberg, & D. J. Cohen (Eds.), *Understanding other minds: Perspectives from autism* (pp. 10–39). New York: Oxford University Press.

Westby, C. E. (2000). A scale for assessing development of children's play. In K. Gitlin-Weiner, A. Sandgrund, & C. E. Schaefer (Eds.), *Play diagnosis and assessment* (2nd ed., pp. 131–161). New York: Wiley & Sons.

Wieder, S., & Greenspan, S. I. (2003). Climbing the symbolic ladder in the DIR model through floor time/interactive play. *Autism: International Journal of Research and Practice, 7*(4), 425–435.

Williams, D. (1992). *Nobody nowhere: The extraordinary autobiography of an autistic.* New York: Times Books.

Williams, E. (2003). A comparative review of early forms of object-directed play and parent–infant play in typical infants and young children with autism. *Autism: The International Journal of Research and Practice, 7*(4), 361–377.

Williams, E., Costall, A., & Reddy, V. (1999). Children with autism experience problems with both objects and people. *Journal of Autism and Developmental Disorders, 29*(5), 367–378.

Williams, E., Reddy, V., & Costall, A. (2001). Taking a closer look at functional play in children with autism. *Journal of Autism and Developmental Disorders, 31*(1), 67–77.

Wimmer, H., & Perner, J. (1983). Beliefs about beliefs: Representation and constraining function of wrong beliefs in young children's understanding of deception. *Cognition, 13*, 103–128.

Wing, L., & Gould, J. (1979). Severe impairments of social interaction and associated abnormalities in children: Epidemiology and classification. *Journal of Autism and Developmental Disorders, 9*, 11–29.

Wing, L., Gould, J., Yeates, S. R., & Brierly, L. M. (1977). Symbolic play in severely mentally retarded and autistic children. *Journal of Child Psychology and Psychiatry, 18*, 167–178.

Wolfberg, P. J. (1988). *Integrated play groups for children with autism and related disorders.* Unpublished master's thesis, San Francisco State University.

Wolfberg, P. J. (1994). Case illustrations of emerging social relations and symbolic activity in children with autism through supported peer play. *Dissertation Abstracts International, 55*(11), 3476A. (UMI No. 9505068)

Wolfberg, P. J. (1995a). Supporting children with autism in play groups with typical peers: A description of a model and related research. *International Play Journal, 3*, 38–51.

Wolfberg, P. J. (1995b). Enhancing children's play. In K. A. Quill (Eds.), *Teaching children with autism: Strategies to enhance communication and socialization* (pp. 193–218). Albany, NY: Delmar.

Wolfberg, P. J. (2003). *Peer play and the autism spectrum: The art of guiding children's socialization and imagination (Integrated Play Groups Field Manual).* Shawnee, KS: Autism Asperger.

Wolfberg, P. J. (2004). Guiding children on the autism spectrum in peer play: Translating theory and research into effective and meaningful practice. *The Journal of Developmental and Learning Disorders*, 8, 7–25.

Wolfberg, P. J. (2005). Play! It's more than just a button on the remote: Including children on the autism spectrum in the culture of childhood. *Autism Spectrum Quarterly*, 2, 8–12.

Wolfberg, P. J. (2008). Including children with autism in the culture of play with peers. In C. Forlin & J. M.-G. Lion (Eds.), *Reforms, inclusion, and teacher education: Towards a new era of special education in the Asia-Pacific region*. London: Routledge.

Wolfberg, P. J., LePage, P., & Cooke, E. (in press). Innovations in teacher education for inclusive education. *International Journal for Whole Schooling*.

Wolfberg, P. J., McCracken, H., & Tuchel, T. (2008). Fostering peer play and friendships: Creating a culture of inclusion. In K. Buron & P. J. Wolfberg (Eds.), *Learners on the autism spectrum: Preparing highly qualified educators* (pp. 182–207). Shawnee Mission, KS: Autism Asperger.

Wolfberg, P. J., & Schuler, A. L. (1992). *Integrated Play Groups: Final report* (Contract #HO86D90016). Washington, DC: United States Department of Education, Office of Special Education Division.

Wolfberg, P. J., & Schuler, A. L. (1993). Integrated Play Groups: A model for promoting the social and cognitive dimensions of play. *Journal of Autism and Developmental Disorders*, 23(3), 1–23.

Wolfberg, P. J. & Schuler, A.L. (1999). Fostering peer interaction, imaginative play, and spontaneous language in children with autism. *Child Language Teaching and Therapy Journal*, 15(1), 41–52.

Wolfberg, P. J., & Schuler, A. L. (2006). Promoting social reciprocity and symbolic representation in children with ASD: Designing quality peer play interventions. In T. Charman & W. Stone (Eds.), *Social and communication development in Autism Spectrum Disorders* (pp. 180–219). New York: Guilford Press.

Wolfberg, P., Turiel, E., & DeWitt, M. (in preparation). *Integrated Play Groups: Promoting symbolic play, social engagement, and communication with peers across settings in children with autism*. Autism Speaks Treatment Grant (Funded 2008–2011).

Wolfberg, P. J., Zercher, C., Lieber, J., Capell, K., Matias, S. G., Hanson, M., & Odom, S. (1999). "Can I play with you?" Peer culture in inclusive preschool programs. *Journal for the Association of Persons with Severe Handicaps*, 24(2), 69–84.

World Health Organization. (1992). *The ICD-10 international statistical classification of diseases and related health problems*. Geneva: Author.

Yang, T., Wolfberg, P .J., Wu, S., & Hwu, P. (2003). Supporting children on the autism spectrum in peer play at home and school: Piloting the Integrated Play Groups model in Taiwan. *Autism: The International Journal of Research and Practice*, 7(4), 437–453.

Zercher, C., Hunt, P., Schuler, A. L., & Webster, J. (2001). Increasing joint attention, play, and language through peer supported play. *Autism: The International Journal of Research and Practice*, 5, 374–398.

Zigler, E., Singer, D., & Bishop-Josef, S. (Eds.). (2004). *Children's play: The roots of reading*. Washington, DC: Zero to Three Press.

Index

120721

About the Author

Pamela Wolfberg, PhD is associate professor of special education and director of the autism spectrum graduate program (Project Mosaic) at San Francisco State University. She earned her doctorate in 1994 from the University of California, Berkeley, where she received a distinguished award for outstanding doctoral dissertation. Her research and practice are centered on peer relations, play and imagination, and childhood culture as related to the social inclusion of children on the autism spectrum. As originator of the Integrated Play Groups model and founder of the Autism Institute on Peer Relations and Play, she leads efforts to develop inclusive peer play programs worldwide. She has published extensively in peer-reviewed journals and academic texts focused on these topics. She serves as principal investigator on major research and training grants and as associate editor for *Autism: International Journal of Research and Practice*. She has an active agenda as an invited international speaker and is the recipient of several eminent awards for her scholarship, research, and service to the community. For more information, visit www.wolfberg.com or www.autisminstitute.com.